51 Chess Openings

For Beginners

D0430148

About the Author

Life Master Bruce Alberston is a well-known teacher and trainer in New York. He's written and narrated the CD-Rom, *Quick Kills on the Chessboard* and is the author of the bestselling *Chess Mazes*. For Cardoza Publishing, he and Fred Wilson have collaborated on *303 Tricky Chess Mates*, *303 Tricky Chess Tactics*, *303 Tricky Chess Puzzles*, *303 More Tricky Chess Puzzles*, and *202 Checkmates for Children*.

51 Chess Openings
For Beginners

Bruce Alberston

Cardoza Publishing

GAMBLER'S BOOK CLUB

Get all your gambling books at Gambler's Book Club in Las Vegas, and enjoy the world's largest selection of gambling books, software, and information—more than 3,000 titles in stock! Also books on chess and other board games.

www.gamblersbookclub.com

FREE POKER & GAMING MAGAZINES!
www.cardozabooks.com

Sign up now to read all about the exciting world of poker, gambling, and online gaming. Our free online magazines are packed with tips, expert strategies, tournament schedules and results, gossip, news, contests, polls, prepublication book discounts, free-money bonuses for online sites, words of wisdom from the world's top experts and authorities, and much more! And what's best—it's FREE! Visit us now!

Cardoza Publishing is the foremost gaming and gambling publisher in the world with a library of more than 200 up-to-date and easy-to-read books and strategies. These authoritative works are written by the top experts in their fields and with more than 10,000,000 books in print, represent the best-selling and most popular gaming books anywhere.

2011 PRINTING

Copyright © 2007 by Bruce Alberston
All Rights Reserved

Library of Congress Catalog Number: 2007921665
ISBN 10: 1-58042-212-8   ISBN 13: 978-1-58042-212-3

Visit our website or write for a full list of Cardoza products.

CARDOZA PUBLISHING

P.O. Box 98115, Las Vegas, NV 89193
Toll-Free Phone (800)577-WINS
email: cardozabooks@aol.com

www.cardozabooks.com

Table of Contents

 **Introduction**

This is a chess openings book for players who are just starting out. I assume you know the moves and rules, most of them anyway, but not a whole lot more. You'll learn the names of the openings, the first five moves, and get to see at least six diagrams so you can play the openings comfortably and confidently.

The idea is to get a feel for where the pieces go, how they come out and in what order, how they link up with friendly forces, and where they stand in conjunction with the fight for the center.

You also get move by move comments explaining the reasons for the moves and their function. Sometimes the moves are strategic, as with pawn moves which gather center space or open lines of development for the pieces. Other times, the moves are tactical, usually White attacking something and Black defending or else counterattacking. Rest assured, there's always a reason.

Finally, the layout of the book is alphabetical for easy reference. Knowledge of any one opening does not depend on any other opening. Since each opening stands on its own, you can pick up the book and start anywhere that interests you.

This book will show you what the chess openings look like. Enjoy!

Standard Symbols and Abbreviations

K or ♔	stands for king
Q or ♕	stands for queen
R or ♖	stands for rook
B or ♗	stands for bishop
N or ♘	stands for knight
P or ♙	stands for pawn although in practice the "P" is rarely used.
x	stands for a capture
—	the dash stands for moves to
0-0	stands for kingside castling
0-0-0	stands for queenside castling
†	stands for check
#	mate stands for mate or checkmate
...	three dots following a move number means it's a Black move. For example, 2...d6 indicates Black's second move was to bring his pawn to d6.
/Q	means promotion of a pawn to a queen.
/N	means promotion of a pawn to a knight
/R	means promotion of a pawn to a rook
/B	means promotion of a pawn to a bishop
!	means a very good move
!!	means a brilliant move
?	means a bad move
??	means a losing blunder
!? or ?!	is a mixture good and bad
1-0	White wins
0-1	Black wins
½-½	draw or tie game

My First Openings

I recall how my own early experience was spent getting used to the movement of the pieces while learning to perform (and fend off) the four move checkmate. A typical game ran:

1. **e4** **e5**
2. **Bc4** **Bc5**
3. **Qh5** **...**

White's queen and bishop line up to attack the weak f7-point, next to the king.

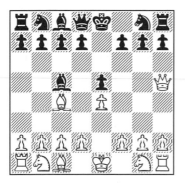

This went unnoticed. Still, the attack on the e5-pawn was spotted. So...

3. ... **d6??**
4. **Qxf7#** **1-0**

Guarding e5 didn't help. Checkmate in four moves.

A bit later I discovered I could also mate from the Black side of the board.

1. **e4** **e5**
2. **Nc3** **Bc5**
3. **Bc4** **Qf6**

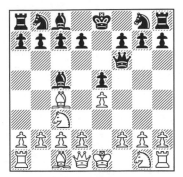

4. Nd5??   Qxf2#   0-1

And so with this double-barreled Scholar's Mate Attack, I was able to rack up a terrific score against my fellow club mates.

Only gradually did it percolate into my head that such fantastic success was possible mainly because my victims were largely beginners. The combined attack of queen and bishop on the f7 (f2) squares was just a little beyond their capacities at the time. And if you can't pick up a one move mate threat, you're in trouble.

The Troxell brothers most certainly were not beginners. Their dad, a former city champion, had imparted some of his chess wisdom to the offspring. And it took. Against the Troxell's, the four move checkmate had no chance of success. By the simple expedient of bringing out their kingside knight they put

an end to the story. Scholar's Mate became a fairy tale.

1.	e4	e5
2.	Bc4	Nf6

Me Versus Troxell Brother

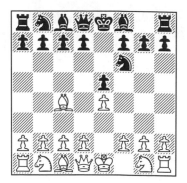

Now 3.Qh5? loses the queen to 3...Nxh5 (that happened). And as for 3.Qf3, it's strictly a wish move. Black keeps his knight at f6 and there's no way for the queen to penetrate to f7.

Clearly the four move checkmate idea was too crude to be effective against advanced players. Something more sophisticated was needed and that meant learning some real openings.

The idea that there might just be such things as real openings came to me as a revelation. Then, acting on a hunch, I made a quick trip to the public library where my suspicions were confirmed.

In the books on display were tons of chess openings, all with weird, unfamiliar names that I had never heard of before. And camouflaging the opening moves was something called English Descriptive Notation.

Tediously I picked up what English Descriptive was all about and then latched on to the Italian Game. The notation read: 1.P-K4 pawn to king four, 1...P-K4 pawn to king four; 2.N-KB3 knight to king-bishop three, 2...N-QB3 knight to queen-bishop three; 3.B-QB4 bishop to queen-bishop four etc. Converting to Algebraic, the universally used form today:

1.	e4	e5
2.	Nf3	Nc6
3.	Bc4	...

The two main branches of the Italian are (1) 3...Bc5, Giuoco Piano and (2) 3...Nf6, Two Knights' Defense. In my games, nobody played 3...Bc5 (except me when I was Black). Everyone went with the knight move...

3. ...   Nf6

I answered with the book move.

4. Ng5   ...

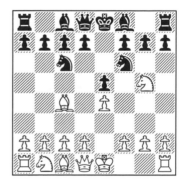

And a not too subtle attack on f7. As in the early days of the Scholar's Mate, once again I was able to obtain a two piece attack on f7, which for an inexperienced player, was not so easy to parry at the board.

Typical was 4...h6? 5.Nxf7 with a fork on queen and rook. And yes, half the time I got the queen. On occasion someone might hit on the best defense...

4. ...   d5

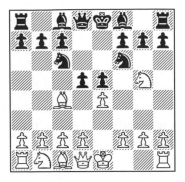

...intercepting the diagonal of the bishop. I had to take.

5. exd5   ...

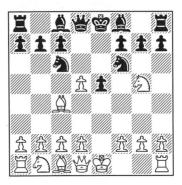

Now unless you knew some Two Knights' opening theory, you would never hit on the book move, 5...Na5. You would play the most natural move in the position and recover your pawn.

5. ...   Nxd5?!

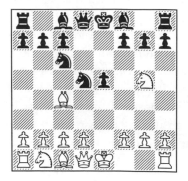

Running right into the Fried Liver Attack.

6. Nxf7!?   ...

A knight sacrifice to draw the Black king out into the open board.

6. ...   Kxf7

He has to accept.

7. Qf3†   ...

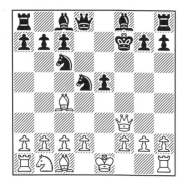

This was a combined attack on the king and knight which I knew something about while my opponents did not. For instance, I knew to answer 7...Ke6 (the best move as it guards the d5-knight) with 8.Nc3, attacking the pinned knight, and obtaining a dangerous attack thanks to Black's exposed king.

But in the early days, nobody ever got that far. Black would play king back to his starting square and I would recover my knight.

7. ...   Ke8
8. Bxd5   ...

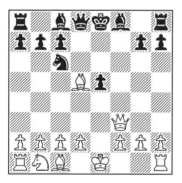

Lo and behold I was threatening a familiar mating finish. In fact, my game with Joe Seng ended after 8... Nd4?? 9.Qf7 mate. The four move checkmate in nine moves. You shouldn't throw the old stuff away completely because you never can tell when you might use it again.

For me the Italian Game was the initiation of opening study and gradually, one opening at a time, the vale of mystery began to lift. After the Italian came the Lopez, the various gambits, followed by the asymmetrical replies to e4. Then the big switch to Queen Pawn openings, Indian Defenses, and the even more obscure flank openings. The process generated excitement, for as soon as I learned of a brand new opening I was determined to try it out in practice.

In this way, over the course of several years, I went through all the different openings: the good, the bad, and the ugly. Among the latter are some truly horrible defenses for which I developed a certain affection. An example of a guilty pleasure was the discredited Damiano's Defense.

1. e4   e5
2. Nf3   f6

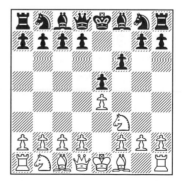

This one is so bad that it doesn't deserve a listing among the 51 openings selected for this book. We should also mention that Portuguese apothecary and writer Damiano, neither invented nor recommended this defense. Rather he condemned it but his name got stuck to it anyway.

Which bring us to the topic of how the chess openings got their names.

HOW OPENINGS ARE NAMED

Basically, names of the chess opening fall into one of three categories.

1. Names of players who brought attention to the opening. In some cases these also happen to be the inventors (or re-inventors) but mostly they are the players who popularized the opening by playing it repeatedly in top notch competition.

2. Geographic areas, mostly cities or countries where the opening first gained attention. These all happen to be in Europe because that's where the modern game got underway and that's where all the major openings got

baptized. Variations within an opening date from a later, more global period. By the early 20th century you can find lines like the Rio de Janeiro Variation of the Ruy Lopez. And since Ruy Lopez was a Spanish priest the whole opening is called the Spanish Game in many quarters. Yes, multiple names for the same opening adds to the confusion.

3. Description of what's happening on the chess board. These descriptions will vary somewhat in texture. You might not glean anything from the term Indian Defense unless you know in advance that Black responds to 1.d4 with 1...Nf6 and (usually) a fianchetto (flanking) of one of his bishops.

In a gambit someone sacrifices a pawn for positional considerations and what he hopes will be full compensation. If the opening is named Four Knights, you expect to see two Black and two White knights developed before any of the other pieces. And you'd be right.

Some Opening Ideas

So far we've looked at how various openings have different names, moves, and ideas. But, in fact, all the openings have certain basic objectives in common. Call them the fundamental principles of opening play. We'll keep the list short.

1. The Center
2. Development
3. King Safety

The Center

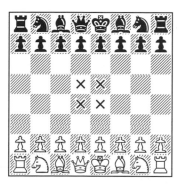

The "X's" show the four squares in the middle of the board, or the **center.** Every good opening move is designed to have some bearing on the center, the hub of initial activity. You're not going to be able to control all four center squares but you do want your fair share. Say you control two of the squares while contesting the other two. That's a pretty good bargain. And likely, your opponent will probably being aiming for the same.

Development means bringing your officers off the home rank into the game. You physically take a piece off the back row and put it in contact with a center square.

You have eight pieces on the home rank and you want to move seven of them: two knights, two bishops, the queen, and the two rooks.

The king stays back for reasons of safety. You don't want the king in the midst of the fighting, so you castle and hide him.

You can add a fourth element if you like, threats. These will directed against the uncastled king or any of the other pieces that may be exposed. They fall under the heading of tactics and apply to all three phases of the game—opening, middle game, and end game. You just have to deal with tactics as they arise. They are not strictly an opening phenomenon.

THE IDEAL OPENING

You're never going to get the ideal opening but you might get close. Let's see what it looks like when Black lets White have his way by moving his knight back and forth from its original position, in effect, having no development at all.

1. e4   Nc6
2. d4   Nb8

Moving out the two center pawns is an excellent way to start. They not only control important squares but they also release the pieces.

Black's moves with his knight are pointless, as are his subsequent moves.

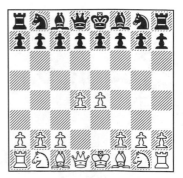

3. Nf3   Nf6
4. Nc3   Ng8

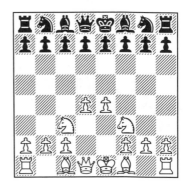

White has furthered his development by bringing out his knights. Note how each knight is in contact with a center square.

5. Bc4   Nc6
6. Bf4   Nb8

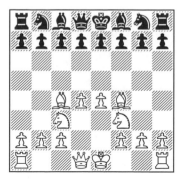

Both bishops are out aiming at center squares in Black's half of the board.

Don't leave your rook in the corner. Bring it into play on one of the center files. When the file opens up the rook will happily be attacking something.

7.	0-0	Na6
8.	Qe2	Nb8

9. ...   **Nf6**

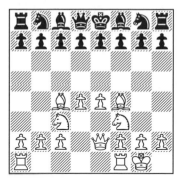

Black continues his waiting strategy which is no strategy at all. White is in full command of the board and ready to cross into enemy territory.

10.	e5	Ng8
11.	d5	h6

White has castled and moved his queen off the back row, making a space for his queenside rook.

9. Radl ...

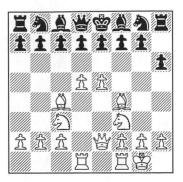

Finally Black decides to make a pawn move and it is useless. He hasn't gotten out of the starting block. Meanwhile White, who has completed his development, is already in the middle game, and ready to commence operations.

His next move makes contact with the enemy pawns and opens the position.

| 12. e6 | dxe6 |
| 13. dxe6 | ... |

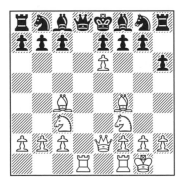

The d-line is clear and the rook attacks the queen. Black covers by blocking the file.

| 13. ... | Nd7 |
| 14. exf7 | mate |

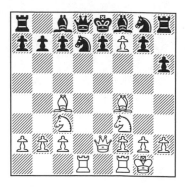

The ideal chess opening has triumphed.

 Alekhine Defense

1. e4 ...

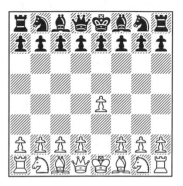

Advancing a center pawn, occupying the square e4.

1. ... Nf6

The characteristic move of the Alekhine Defense. Black develops his kingside knight and attacks the undefended e4-pawn.

2. e5 ...

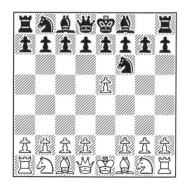

The pawn defends itself by moving forward, attacking the f6-knight.

2. ...   Nd5

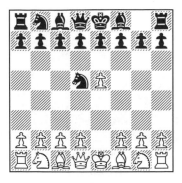

The threatened knight moves away from the pawn attack and into the center. Here the knight has a fine radius of attack. White's next move shows that he wants Black's knight out of the center.

3. c4   ...

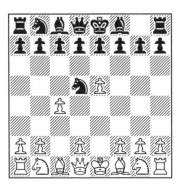

Yet another pawn attack on the enemy knight, this time to force it out of the center and towards the wing.

3. ...   Nb6

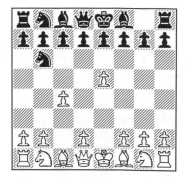

The knight withdraws. At present the knight is safe. If White ventures forth with c4-c5, the knight can return to d5.

4. d4   ...

White advances his queen's pawn, occupying d4 and supporting his e5 pawn. He plans a broad pawn front in the middle of the board.

4. ...   d6

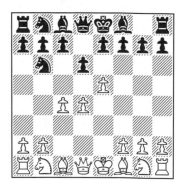

Finally Black gets to advance one of his center pawns. His idea is to attack the forward pawn at e5 and ultimately break up White's pawn center.

Black takes. On 6.dxe5 he trades queens, while on 6.fxe4 he will try to exert pressure on the d4-pawn, by 6...c5 or by 6...Nc6.

5. f4   ...

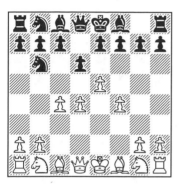

This advance is designed to bolster e5 and build a huge front of pawns in mid board. For obvious reasons, this whole line is known as the "four pawns attack."

5. ...   dxe5

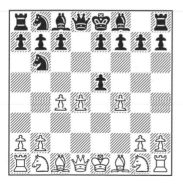

2 Benko Gambit

1. d4 ...   **2. ... Nf6**

The queen pawn games all begin with this move and can go off in many different directions. This means that for the practical player it is important to be flexible, ready to make adjustments as they come up.

The flexible Indian Defense which says absolutely nothing about how Black intends to continue his opening. All we can say at present is that the move is good. It develops a piece and attacks important squares in the center.

2. c4 ...

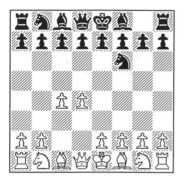

Played in standard fashion. The c-pawn moves out in preparation for bringing his knight to c3.

2. ... c5

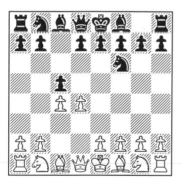

Challenging White in the center and more or less provoking the advance.

3. d5 ...

Moving into Black territory, gathering space in the central zone.

3. ... b5

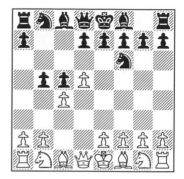

The Benko Counter Gambit. The ideas behind this move are purely positional as Black is going to wind up playing this game a pawn behind.

4. cxb5 ...

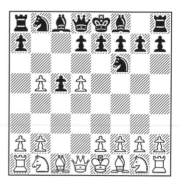

White accepts the gambit.

4. ...	a6

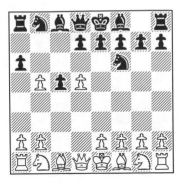

If White does nothing Black gets his pawn back.

5. bxa6 ...

White retains his extra pawn, and Black gets two attacking files on the queenside, the a and b lines.

5. ...	g6

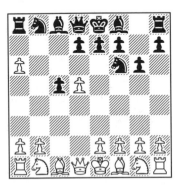

Rightly figuring that the a6-pawn won't run away.

6. Nc3	Bxa6
7. e4	Bxf1
8. Kxf1	d6

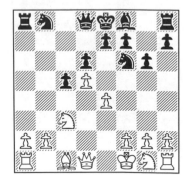

Black plays ...Bg7 and castles. Overall he has a pretty decent game despite one less pawn.

3 Bird's Opening

1. f4 ...

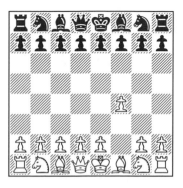

White plays to control the central e5-point with his f-pawn.

1. ... d5

Black stakes his claim to the center, moving his d-pawn out two squares. The pawn occupies d5 and sets up control over e4, a counterweight to White's control of e5. Also, a line is opened for his queenside bishop to come out.

2. e3 ...

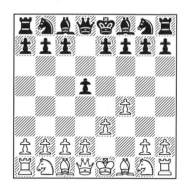

Opens a line for his queen and f1-bishop. In the event that Black plays 2...Nc6, White can contest control of e5 by pinning the knight, 3.Bb5.

2. ...   Nf6

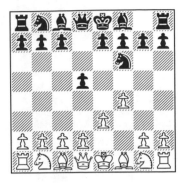

Black develops his kingside knight which together with his d5-pawn adds to the pressure on the e4-square.

3. Nf3   ...

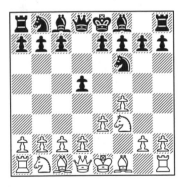

Consistent with the basic idea of the Bird, White brings out his knight so as to add more control to e5.

3. ...   Bg4

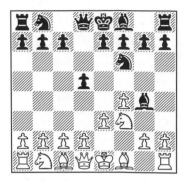

Develops his c8-bishop, in turn pinning the knight, reducing pressure on e5.

4. h3   ...

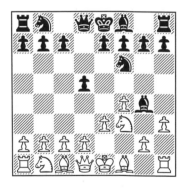

The pin must be attended to. 4.Be2 is possible but the text move, asking the bishop to declare its intentions, is more forcing.

4. ...   Bxf3

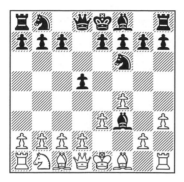

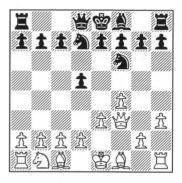

The bishop saves itself from the pawn attack by trading for the f3-knight.

Black brings out his queenside knight and prepares to challenge for control of e5. The position offers about even chances.

5. Qxf3   ...

5. ...   Nbd7

4 Bishop's Opening

1. e4 ...

One of the oldest opening moves, designed to clear a diagonal for the f1-bishop.

1. ... e5

The standard response whereby Black opens the a3-f8 diagonal for his dark-squared bishop.

2. Bc4 ...

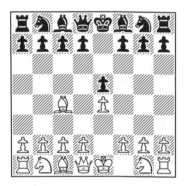

This is the Bishop's Opening. White develops his bishop where it bears down on the central d5-square and also the f7-square, near Black's king.

2. ...   Bc5

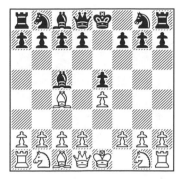

The Black bishop comes out aiming to control the d4-point. In addition the bishop aims at the vulnerable f2 point in White's camp.

3. c3   ...

Challenging Black for control of d4, in fact preparing d2-d4. The alternative 3.Qh5, threatening mate, is considered too crude to be effective. Black easily defends with 3...Qe7 (or Qf6).

3. ...   Nf6

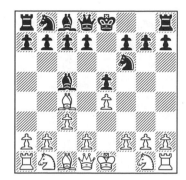

The rule is that when White plays c2-c3, Black should immediately attack the undefended e4-pawn. That's what he's doing.

4. d4   ...

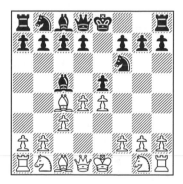

White advances his d-pawn and attacks the enemy bishop. Also, the e5-pawn is under fire, so it's a double attack by the pawn.

4. ...   exd4

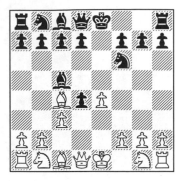

5. ...   d5

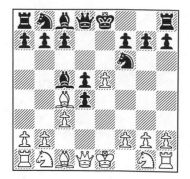

Black captures the d-pawn before it can do real damage, In the event of the recapture 5.cxd4 Black gives a bishop check at b4.

Black counterattacks. "If you take my knight, I take your bishop."

5. e5   ...

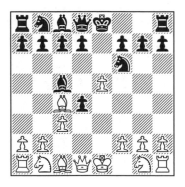

Advancing on the knight. If the knight gives ground, moving say to e4, White intends to recapture cxd4.

5 Bogoljubov's Defense

1. d4 ...

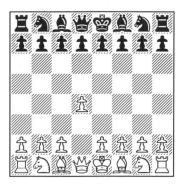

White follows the standard strategy of placing a pawn in the center. You can do it with your e-pawn or your d-pawn, but you should do it one way or the other.

1. ... Nf6

A most flexible response whereby Black develops his kingside knight and exerts a certain measure of control over e4. We mean by this that if White advances 2.e4? Black can capture.

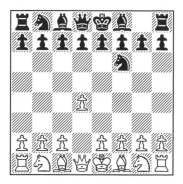

2...Nxe4, winning a pawn for nothing. You control a square when you can capture on that square.

2. c4 ...

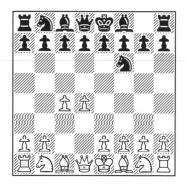

Since he cannot advance his pawn to e4, White tries to pressure d5 with his c-pawn. On 2...d5 White takes 3.cxd5 and Black would have to recapture with a piece, queen or knight, neither of which is all that desirable in the present circumstances.

2. ...   e6

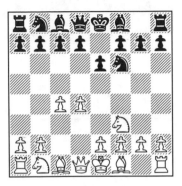

Advancing the pawn to e6 means that on a later ...d7-d5, if White captures cxd5, Black has the option of recapturing with his pawn.

3. Nf3   ...

White brings out his g1-knight, a perfectly good move at this juncture.

3. ...   Bb4†

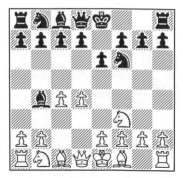

The Bogoljubov. Black takes the opportunity of developing his bishop with check. White must drop whatever he's doing and save his king. Fortunately he has several ways to block at d2. The worst is with the queen. I hope you understand why.

4. Bd2   ...

White blocks with his bishop, in turn threatening the enemy b4-bishop.

4. ...   Bxd2†

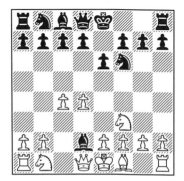

Black saves his bishop by trading it off. Bishop for bishop is an even trade.

5. Qxd2 ...

Recapture with the queen. Why not the b1-knight? Because he can get more value placing it on c3.

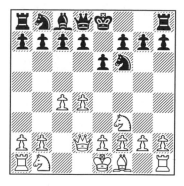

5. ... d5

Black makes his stand in the middle, insuring that in the coming battle he will have his share of central space.

6 Budapest Defense

1. d4   ...

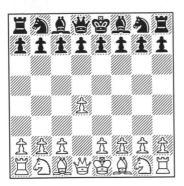

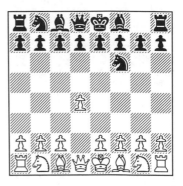

White signals his intent to keep Black under restraint by controlling the e5-square in Black's half of the board. Can you really control a square in the opponent's part of the board at the outset of the game? We will see.

1. ...   Nf6

For the moment Black is happy to develop a piece. He'll worry about e5 after he sees White's next move.

2. c4   ...

To control d5. Otherwise he might have played 2.Nf3, reserving c4 for later.

2. ...   e5

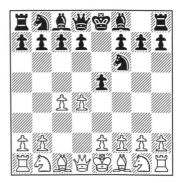

Surprise, Black offers a pawn on the e5-square. This is the cheeky, trappy Budapest Counter Gambit.

3. dxe5 ...

He might as well take. The books note the trap after: 3.d5 Bc5 4.Bg5 Ne4 5.Bxd8?? Bxf2 mate.

The trap after 5...Bxf2#

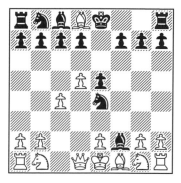

Naturally, White doesn't want to fall into that one.

3. ... Ng4

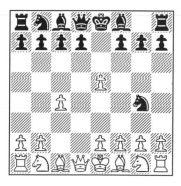

The attacked knight moves out of range, in such a way as to reverse the roles.

4. Bf4 ...

Guards the pawn. He could also give it back, 4.e4 Nxe5 5.f4, chasing the knight and building a big pawn center.

4. ... Nc6

Attacks the e5-pawn with his other knight. White to defend once again.

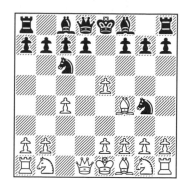

5. Nf3 ...

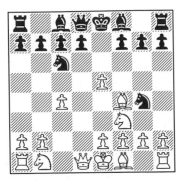

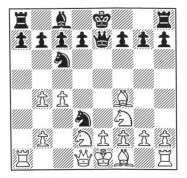

Which is what he does. Now the pawn is twice attacked and twice defended.

Don't fall into that one.

5. ...   Bb4†

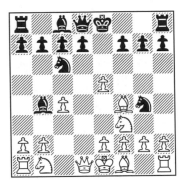

Black gets ready to attack e5 with ...Qe7. The books record the following trap: 6.Nbd2 Qe7 7.a3 Ngxe5 8.axb4?? Nd3 mate.

7 Caro-Kann Defense

1. e4 ...

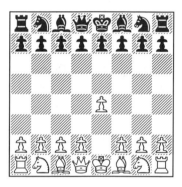

Opens lines for the pieces and establishes influence in the center.

1. ... c6

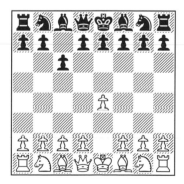

The characteristic move of the Caro-Kann, preparing to advance the d7-pawn to the center.

2. d4 ...

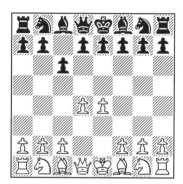

Placing two pawns side by side in the center is an excellent way to start the game.

2. ... d5

Challenges White's grip on the center through this attack on the e4-pawn. If White should take 3.exd5, Black takes back with his c6-pawn.

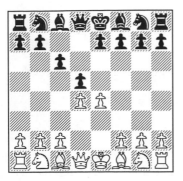

3. Nc3 ...

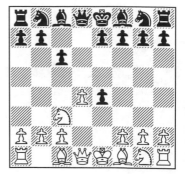

4. Nxe4 ...

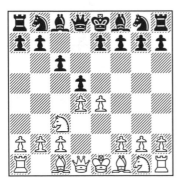

White protects his e4-pawn by bringing out his queenside knight.

White must take back else he's a pawn down for nothing.

3. ... dxe4

Black relieves the central tension by capturing at e4.

4. ...   Nf6

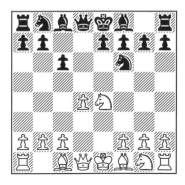

Black continues his assault on White's center, attacking the e4-knight with his own. Another way was to use the bishop, 4...Bf5. Also 4...Nd7 and then 5...Ngf6.

5. Nxf6†   ...

The simplest defense of the e4-knight is to take the Black f6-knight with check.

5. ...   exf6

Black recaptures with his e7-pawn, opening a diagonal for his f8 bishop to come out. The plan is to play the bishop to d6 and then castle. The alternative is 5...gxf6, a totally different kind of structure.

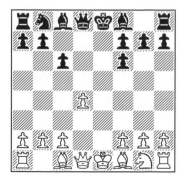

This is the original treatment of the Caro-Kann. Probably White has a slight advantage owing to Black's doubled f-pawns. But it's not much to work with and otherwise Black's game is pretty steady.

Center Counter Defense

1. e4 ...

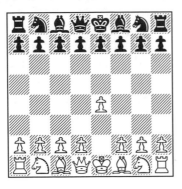

Looking to establish some measure of control over the d5-square.

1. ... d5

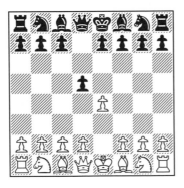

Center Counter, immediately contesting for control of d5 by direct attack on the e4-pawn.

2. exd5 Qxd5

Capture and recapture; a mutual trade of pawns on the contested d5-point.

3. Nc3 ...

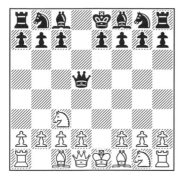

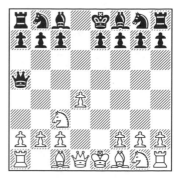

The pawn exchange has lured Black's queen to d5, and the knight develops with gain of time. Where the queen should go is anyone's guess.

Playing into Black's hands to some extent, as the knight is now pinned. All the same, White cannot get by without pushing his d-pawn. It enables him to develop his forces and control center squares.

3. ...   Qa5

4. ...   Nf6

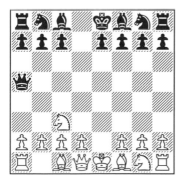

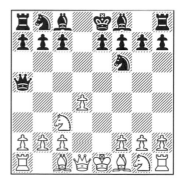

The queen recoils from the threat of the knight. Why to a5? Mainly to pin the knight at c3 after White moves out the queen's pawn.

Developing and continuing the fight for control of the light squares d5 and e4.

4. d4   ...

5. Nf3   ...

Develops the knight, reinforcing control over the points d4 and e5.

5. ... Bg4

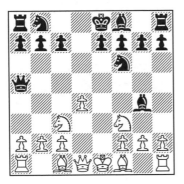

Brings out the light square bishop and pins White's f3-knight. White's first order of business must be to attend to the annoying pin. He can try unpinning by 6.Be2 or perhaps forcibly breaking the pin by 6.h3 Bh5 7.g4. In any case a wide open game ensues.

9 Center Game

1. e4   ...

Advancing the e-pawn two spaces establishes White's position in the center.

1. ...   e5

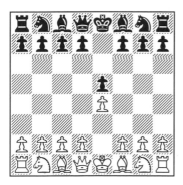

Black in turn establishes his own presence in the center, occupying the e5-point.

2. d4   ...

White plays to destroy the Black e5-pawn which is currently under fire from the d-pawn. The effect is to induce a trade of pawns which serves to open up the middle.

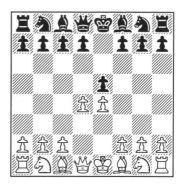

2. ...   exd4

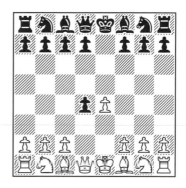

Black exchanges to avoid losing a pawn. The alternative was to guard the pawn somehow, 2...d6 or 2...Nc6. But the trade at d4 is best.

3. Qxd4   ...

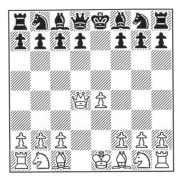

White could gambit a pawn, 3.Nf3 or 3.c3. He recaptures to keep material even. Now he has the characteristic position of the Center Game, queen and pawn in the center.

3. ...   Nc6

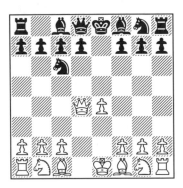

The knight develops with tempo on the queen. She must move again and it's far from clear where to go.

4. Qe3   ...

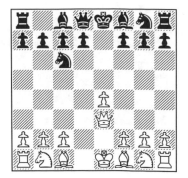

The queen takes up a position of safety behind the e4-pawn. In the event Black advances, 4...d5? White takes, 5.exd5 with discovered check.

4 ...   Nf6

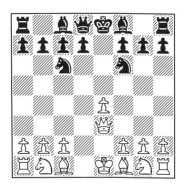

Black brings out his king's knight attacking the central points d5 and e4.

5. Nc3   ...

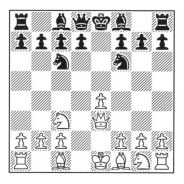

White develops his queenside knight supporting the central points d5 and e4. He's planning to bring out his c1-bishop and then castle queenside.

5. ...   Be7

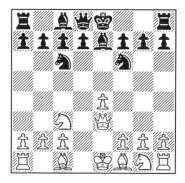

Develops his bishop and readies to castle kingside.

10 Colle System

1. d4 ...

The Colle System is one of the queen pawn openings where White does not play his c-pawn up to c4. And as everyone knows you can't have a queen pawn opening without moving your d2-pawn.

1. ... d5

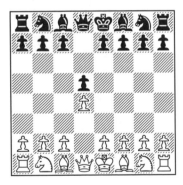

When both sides move their d-pawns two spaces we get a double queen pawn opening. That's what we have here.

2. Nf3 ...

In the Colle, White is in no rush to touch his queen's bishop pawn (c2). Instead he concentrates on bringing out his kingside forces, starting with his king-knight.

2. ... Nf6

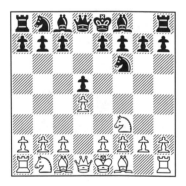

Black plays in similar fashion. Copying White's last move, he develops his g8-knight. If it's good enough for White it should be good enough for Black.

3. e3   ...

Characteristic of the Colle; White opens a path for his f1-bishop to come out. True, this comes at the expense of the c1-bishop whose diagonal has now been closed, but White intends to remedy this state of affairs in the not-too-distant future.

3. ...   e6

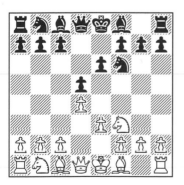

As Black is not under any threat, he is content to copy White's moves for the present. Naturally, Black has some good alternatives in 3... Bf5 and in 3...c5. On 3...Bf5 White makes an adjustment by 4.c4, switching to the Queen's Gambit. And on 3...c5 he has the option of 4.c4 (Queen's Gambit) or 4.c3, still in a Colle.

4. Nbd2   ...

Steady play. The knight comes out to insure control of e4. Note that the knight does not play to c3 where it blocks White's c-pawn. In the Colle, White reserves the option of advancing his c-pawn to c3 to bolster his center pawn at d4.

4. ...   Bd6

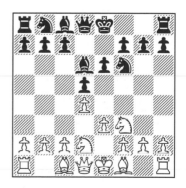

Develops his king bishop and prepares to castle.

5. Bd3 ...

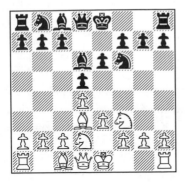

It looks like both sides are playing the same formation. d3 is the natural post for the king bishop. The idea is to liberate the c1-bishop by playing e3-e4.

5. ... 0-0

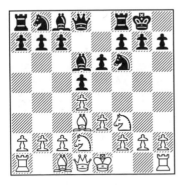

Black is content to castle. He might have tried to pressure White's center through 5...c5 6.c3 Nc6. But Black didn't do that.

1. e4 ...

Opens a line for the f1-bishop.

1. ... e5

Stops the e4-pawn from advancing.

2. d4 ...

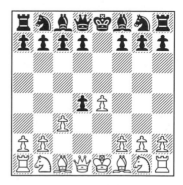

White foregoes recapture 3.Qxd4 (Center Game) and instead offers a gambit to speed his development.

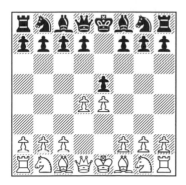

Rips open the center.

2. ... exe4

Captures to avoid losing a pawn.

3. c3 ...

3. ... dxc3

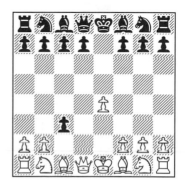

Black accepts the challenge and takes the second pawn. He could have declined with 3...d5.

4. Bc4   ...

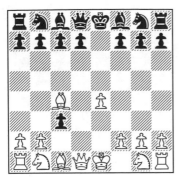

The offer of the third pawn constitutes the full Danish. He could have stopped short and played the half Danish, 4.Nxc3.

4. ...   cxb2

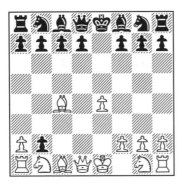

Black keeps taking pawns. He's now three pawns ahead and threatens to take the rook. White better take back.

5. Bxb2   ...

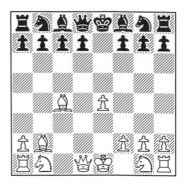

Finally White has to stop and recapture, else he drops a piece. For the two pawns sacrificed he's two bishops ahead in development. Is it enough?

A short game from this position ran 5...Bb4† 6.Nc3 Nf6 7.Ne2 Nxe4 Black is back to three pawns ahead. 8.0-0 Nxc3 9.Nxc3 Bxc3 10.Bxc3 and after 10...0-0 Black seems safe enough.

Analysis: after 10...0-0

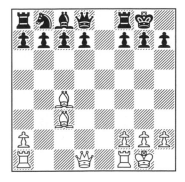

In fact Black is lost after 11.Qg4! g6 12.Qd4, with mate at g7 or h8.

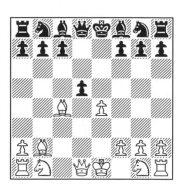

Returning a pawn to get his own pieces out. 6.Bxd5 Nf6 7.Bxf7† Kxf7 8.Qxd8 Bb4† is rated about even.

Analysis after 12. Qd4

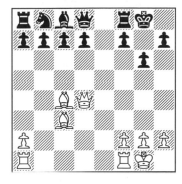

5. ...   d5

12 Dunst Opening

1. Nc3   ...

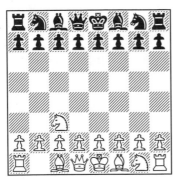

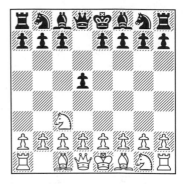

2. e4   ...

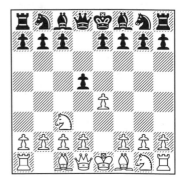

This is a bit off the beaten track but it can't be bad as it develops a piece towards the center. In general, White, thanks to his first move advantage, has some leeway in how he wants to play out his pieces in the early part of the game. This is more so than Black who often has to operate under certain constraints.

1. ...   d5

Since White's initial move is non-threatening Black has some choices. Here the moves ...c5, ...e5, and ...Nf6, can also be played.

Consistent with his first move, White mounts an attack on the point d5. To accumulate threats, you make your forces coordinate as White does here with his e-pawn and knight.

2. ...   d4

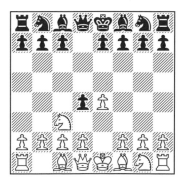

White threatened to gain a pawn so Black had to react. Instead 2... e6 3.d4 would lead to one of the variations of the French Defense. The text is more aggressive, threatening to take the knight.

The knight must run, but not 3.Nd5? e5, and Black threatens to trap the errant knight by ...c7-c6.

3. Nce2   ...

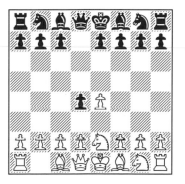

3. ...   e5

The e-pawn comes up to guard its fellow pawn at d4, and to release the f8-bishop. It also keeps the White e4-pawn from advancing any further into Black's camp.

4. Ng3   ...

Clears a path for the f1-bishop and guards e4.

4. ...   Be6

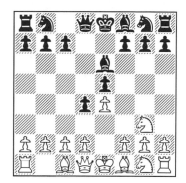

It is clear that White wants to bring his f1-bishop out to c4, and there is no reason why Black should allow it when he can easily prevent this move.

5. d3   ...

Opening the diagonal for the c1-bishop, White aims to advance on the kingside with f2-f4.

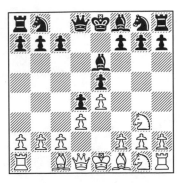

5. ...   Nc6

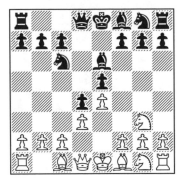

Hindering 6.f4 through the counter 6...Bb4† 7.Bd2 exf4. White can set it up again with 6.a3, stopping the bishop check at b4.

13 Dutch Defense

1. d4   **...**

The Dutch is a defense to White's queen pawn opening, so first we have to get White to move his d2-pawn. That's the purpose of the text.

2. ...   **f5**

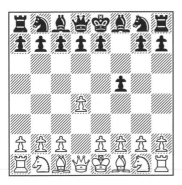

This is the Dutch Defense. Black clamps down on the e4-square using his f pawn. If White insists on playing his pawn up to e4, it costs him a pawn; Black takes 2...fxe4.

2. g3   **...**

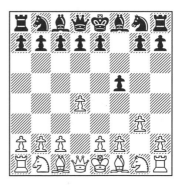

Preparation for Bg2. The text is not that obvious and was arrived at empirically after trying many other moves. Experience has shown that the g3-pawn along with the bishop at g2 helps protect White's king after castling. Not getting mated is a pretty good motive for a move.

2. ...   **Nf6**

Black develops his knight and in conjunction with his f5-pawn continues to clamp down on e4.

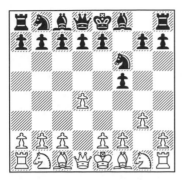

3. Bg2 ...

The consistent follow up to his previous move. A space has been vacated for the bishop to come to g2 and now the bishop goes there. You start something, you finish it. That's logical, consistent chess; that's what you want.

3. ... e6

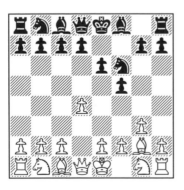

This is one of the turning points of the opening. Black wants to develop his bishop along the a3-f8 diagonal. That's the reason for playing up his e-pawn. If instead he wanted the bishop on the long diagonal, then 3...g6 along with 4...Bg7 would be the choice.

4. Nf3 ...

White's plans c2-c4 but there's no rush. If he plays it too quickly he has to contend with an annoying bishop check at b4.

4. ... Be7

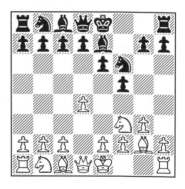

There's no point in 4...Bb4† as then 5.c3 pushes the bishop back.

5. c4 ...

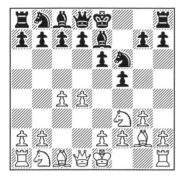

Now White has no objection to the b4-check as it costs Black a tempo. He's already moved his bishop once before.

5. ...   0-0

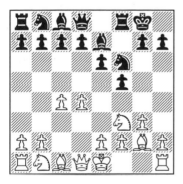

Black gets his king to safety. White will do the likewise on his next turn. Then Black has to make a decision, either 6...d7-d6 or 6...d7-d5. The latter is known as the Stonewall and leads to closed structures requiring lots of patience.

14 English Opening

1. c4 ...

Pushing the c2-pawn, attacking d5, is the characteristic move of the English.

1. ... e5

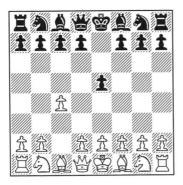

Advancing the e-pawn opens a line for his f8-bishop to come out.

2. Nc3 ...

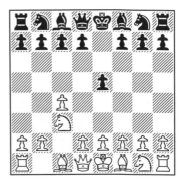

Developing the b1-knight to c3 is consistent with the basic idea of the English, enhancing pressure on d5.

2. ... Nf6

Black develops his kingside knight and in this way counters White's pressure on the light central squares, d5 and e4.

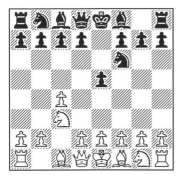

3. Nf3 ...

Developing with a threat on the e5-pawn.

3. ... Nc6

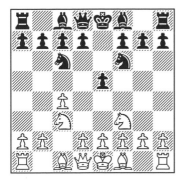

Countering the threat as the c6-knight guards c5.

4. d4 ...

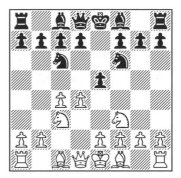

This second attack on the e5-pawn is intended to induce a pawn exchange, opening the d-file from White's end of the board. An open d-file means more White pressure on d5.

4. ... exd4

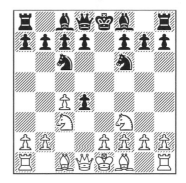

Black exchanges pawns in order not to lose time defending. White has to react as Black is threatening to take the knight on c3. You don't want to lose knights.

59

5. Nxd4 ...

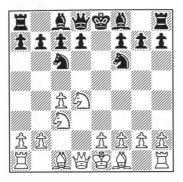

A normal recapture. You take me, I take you back. Now White has a strong knight in the center.

5. ... Bb4

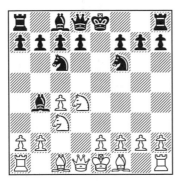

Black develops his dark-squared bishop, clearing out space between his king and rook, preparing to castle kingside. He also pins the c3-knight, part of the overall battle for control of light central squares, which can very well continue 6.Bg5, pinning Black's f6-knight.

1. e4 ...

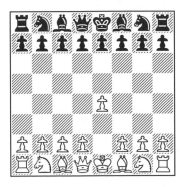

An excellent opening move releasing the queen and f1-bishop from captivity.

1. ... **e5**

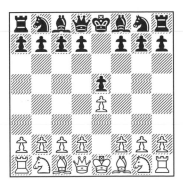

A copy cat reply which influences control of the d4-square. This move also releases the f8-bishop which can now come out along the a3-f8 diagonal.

2. Nf3 ...

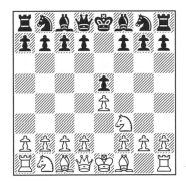

Developing and attacking the e5-pawn which lacks a direct guard.

2. ... **Nc6**

The recommended method of defending the pawn. By bringing out his queen knight, Black aids development.

61

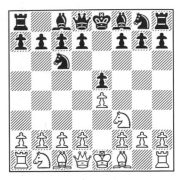

3. Bc4 ...

Aiming the bishop at d5 as well as the sensitive f7.

3. ... Bc5

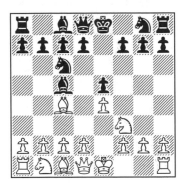

Black develops his bishop in symmetrical fashion. The immediate aim is to control the d4-point where Black has trained three of his units.

4. b4 ...

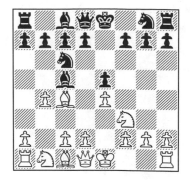

This surprise attack on the bishop is the identifying move of the Evans Gambit. Its immediate import, apart from threatening to take the bishop, is to distract it from d4.

4. ... Bxb4

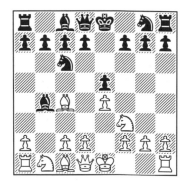

Black accepts the gambit pawn. And why not? It looks like it's for free.

5. c3   **...**

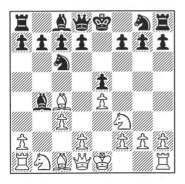

The c-pawn comes up and once again Black's bishop is attacked. That's the tactical point. The strategic point, however, is to gain control over d4.

Where does the bishop go? Practically every square has been tried including f8.

5. ...   **Bc5**

The bishop moves out of danger and returns to its previous post. Likely after d2-d4 the bishop will have to move again, but that choice can be made later.

16 Four Knights' Game

| 1. e4 | ... | 2. Nf3 | ... |

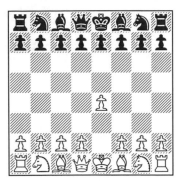

One of the main opening moves.

1. ... e5

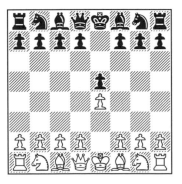

Keeps parity in the center.

Developing his knight with an attack on the enemy central pawn at e5.

2. ... Nc6

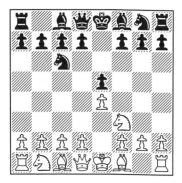

Defends with his queenside-knight.

3. Nc3 ...

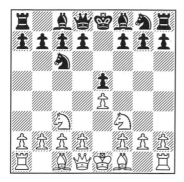

Following the rule "knights before bishops."

3. ... Nf6

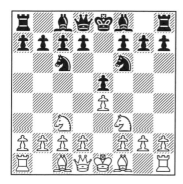

Completes the basic opening. We can now see why it's called the Four Knights' Game.

4. Bb5 ...

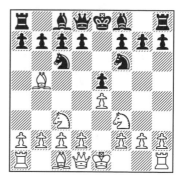

This is the Spanish version. The bishop attacks the c6-knight which in turn defends the e5-pawn.

4. ... Bb4

Black continues symmetry, counterattacking the e4-pawn by threatening to remove the defender at c3.

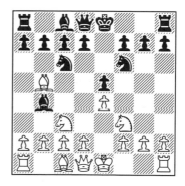

5. 0-0 ...

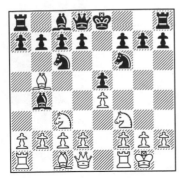 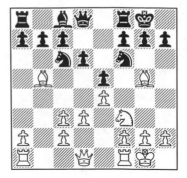

Before undertaking any operations, White first insures the safety of his king by castling. Black next move is in the same mold.

The game goes on.

5. ...   0-0

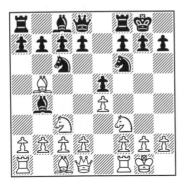

The rest goes 6.d3 d6 7.Bg5 and now probably 7...Bxc3 (not allowing Nd5) 8.bxc3 etc.

 French Defense

1. e4 ...

A territorial move gaining space in the center and maybe additional space if his pawn is allowed to advance to e5.

1. ... e6

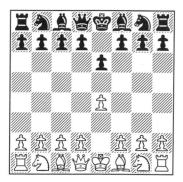

An all-purpose asymmetrical reply which knocks out any opening schemes White may have had in mind. The game will be played in Black's court, in a solid opening of his own choosing.

2. d4 ...

The most natural response. White is not threatened with anything so he uses his turn to gain further ground in the center. Any time you can put two pawns side by side in the center, do it.

2. ... d5

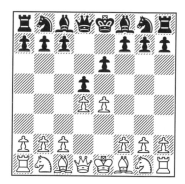

The logical follow up to his first move. (1...e6 without 2...d5 is not a French). Black attacks the White central formation and threatens to capture the undefended e4-pawn.

3. e5 ...

This is just one of several ways to avoid losing a pawn; 3.exd5 and 3.Nc3 also come to consideration. White advances his e-pawn while crossing into enemy territory, preventing Black from developing his knight to its natural square at f6.

3. ...   c5

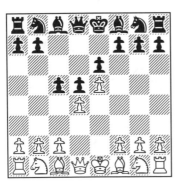

The interlocking of central pawns forms a chain and the approved strategy for Black is to attack the base of White's chain. That's the purpose of Black's last. If the d4-pawn is removed then the e5-pawn could prove weak since it lacks its natural support.

4. c3   ...

To strengthen the queen pawn. Should Black take on d4, White recaptures cxd4 maintaining the integrity of the chain.

4. ...   Nc6

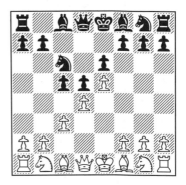

Enough of pawn moves. Black develops a piece, his knight pressing against the enemy d4 and e5 pawns.

5. Nf3   ...

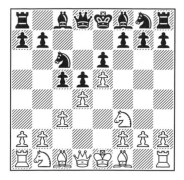

White too has had his fill of pawn moves. For example 5.f4 to support e5, is one pawn move too many. Here the same task can be accomplished by bringing out his kingside knight which also bolsters the pawn at d4.

5. ...   Qb6

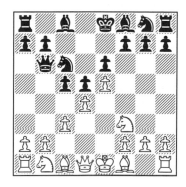

The early queen move is acceptable as it conforms with the needs of the position. From b6, the queen pressures d4 and limits White's possibilities.

18 Giuoco Piano

1. e4   ...

Clears diagonal lines for bishop and queen to come out. Normally the bishop gets out quickly while the queen stays back.

1. ...   e5

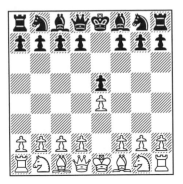

Has the same goals as e4 does for White, opening lanes for the bishop and queen to be developed.

2. Nf3   ...

Developing the g1-knight with attack on the e5-pawn. This attack cannot be ignored, else White gains a pawn for nothing and therefore limits Black's options.

2. ...   Nc6

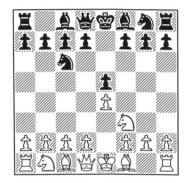

Guarding the e5-pawn with a developing move; the queenside knight gets into the game.

3. Bc4   ...

From c4 the bishop bears down on the central point d5. In addition, by clearing out f1 and g1, White prepares to castle kingside.

3. ...   Bc5

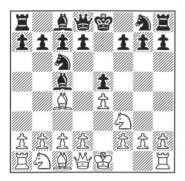

Brings the dark-squared bishop to where it observes the central point d4. In this way the bishop coordinates with the e5-pawn and the c6-knight, all of which attack d4.

4. d3   ...

Secures e4 and opens a pathway for his c1-bishop.

4. ...   Nf6

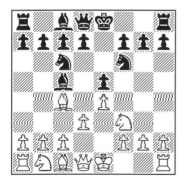

Develops his g8-knight to its most active square, striking at the central points d5 and e4. Also Black is ready to castle if the need arises. If 5.Ng5 0-0, the f7-point is fully protected by king and rook.

5. Nc3   ...

Time to bring out the queenside pieces. The knight comes to its optimal square guarding e4 and looking to strike at d5.

5. ...   d6

Black shores up his central c5-pawn in the most solid fashion: He guards it with another pawn. In addition, the advance of the d7-pawn opens a pathway for the c8-bishop to come out.

The resulting position after Black's fifth move is one of perfect symmetry. But note that symmetry cannot be continued indefinitely. If Black doesn't vary he can go down very quickly. We cite an example: 6.0-0 0-0 7.Bg5 Bg4 8.Nd5 Nd4 9.Qd2! Qd7? 10.Bxf6 Bxf3 11.Ne7† check breaks symmetry.

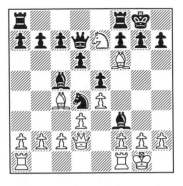

11. ...Kh8 12.Bxg7†! Kxg7 13.Qg5† Kh8 14.Qf6#

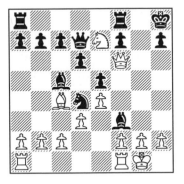

19 Grünfeld Defense

1. d4 ...

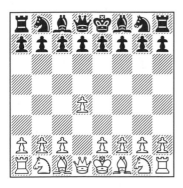

Everyone has a favorite opening move, either e4 or d4. But to find out which one you really like, you have to try out both. Here White tries out the move of the d-pawn. Maybe he'll like it.

1. ... Nf6

The characteristic move of the Indian Defenses. The flexible knight move says nothing at all about how Black intends to arrange his pawns. That keeps White in the dark.

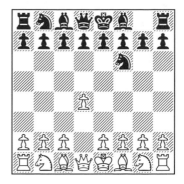

2. c4 ...

White is less shy about showing his colors and the c-pawn boldly advances towards the center. The idea is that if a Black pawn shows up at d5, White can take it, thereby gaining pawn superiority in the middle.

2. ... g6

Nor does this move tell us much about how Black intends to handle his center pawns. All we can gather from ...g7-g6 is that Black wants to put his bishop on g7, striking at the dark squares on the long diagonal.

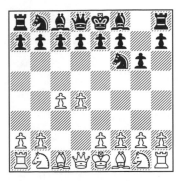

3. Nc3   ...

White is not deflected by Black's cat-and-mouse game and directs his forces towards the center. The intention seems to be e2-e4 on the next move.

3. ...   d5

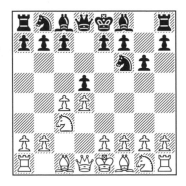

This is Grünfeld's startling advance, which took the chess community by surprise in the early 1920's. Everyone thought it was a positional mistake, but the Austrian

Grandmaster was the first to realize otherwise.

4. cxd5   ...

We know why the pawn came to c4 in the first place, to take a Black pawn when it shows up at d5.

4. ...   Nxd5

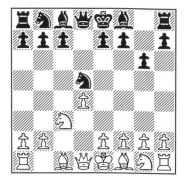

The best recapture. But now the knight on d5 is no longer controlling e4. That allows White's next move.

5. e4   ...

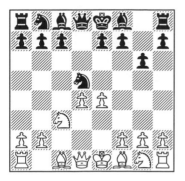

Forcing the situation by attacking Black's knight.

5. ...   Nxc3

Black saves his knight by trading for the enemy knight. True, after 6.bxc3, White has the ideal pawn center, but what Grünfeld understood is that Black can attack the White center with ...Bg7 and ...c5, with kingside castling thrown in somewhere. In any case, the Grünfeld is still going strong at the beginning of the 21st century.

20 Hungarian Defense

1. e4 ...

The pieces on the home rank must be brought into play. To do this they must first be released by line opening pawn moves. That is the purpose of the text, to open lines for the queen and f1-bishop.

1. ... e5

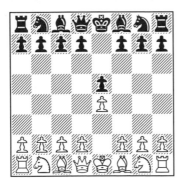

With this advance Black insures himself equal play in the center of the board, at the same time opening squares for his queen and king bishop to come out.

2. Nf3 ...

Black has provided White with an object of attack at e5. The knight hones in threatening to take Black's pawn for nothing.

2. ... Nc6

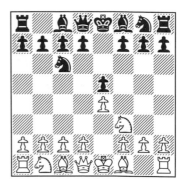

Black counters by bringing up his b8-knight to guard e5 so that the transaction 3.Nxe5? Nxe5 leaves White down a piece for a pawn.

3. Bc4 ...

White foregoes further attack on e5 for the moment and concentrates on getting a new piece into action. The bishop bears down on the f7-

pawn and in the event of say, 3... Nf6, White may continue a further attack on f7 with 4.Ng5.

3. ...   Be7

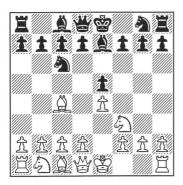

On the more aggressive looking 3...Bc5 the bishop could be harassed by the White pawns, 4.c3 and 5.d4, or by the Evans Gambit 4.b4. In both cases, complications arise that Black may not be familiar with. The solid text move avoids these unpleasant contingencies and emerges as the Hungarian Defense.

4. d4   ...

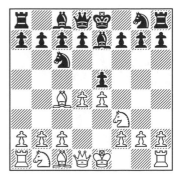

The conservative bishop placement at e7 prompts White to seize the initiative with a double attack on e5.

4. ...   d6

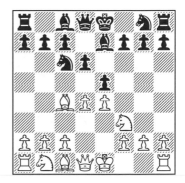

Solidly guarding e5, maintaining his posture in the center. The alternative 4...exd4 5.Nxd4 concedes White center space.

5. dxe5   ...

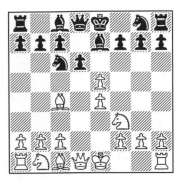

The trade on e5 is just one of several lines for White. 5.Nc3 and 5.d5 also have their supporters. The idea is to keep the position open, looking to take advantage of White's more active piece placement.

5. ...   dxe5

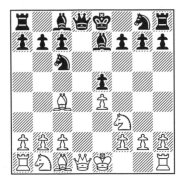

Recaptures with his pawn in order to have stability in the center. True, after 6.Qxd8† Bxd8, White exerts some light pressure, but all the same, Black's game is readily defensible.

 King's Gambit Accepted

1. e4 ...

The starting move for all king pawn openings and the majority of gambits.

1. ... e5

Double king pawn reply. Anything else by Black is asymmetrical and in the old days was considered a wimp out. Today, thanks to political correctness, asymmetry and wimps are in.

2. f4 ...

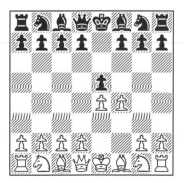

The King's Gambit; Black can accept or decline. The idea is to knock out Black's e5-pawn (lure it to f4) so that White can expand in the center with d2-d4.

2. ... exf4

Black accepts the challenge and takes the pawn. Now White can't very well continue 3.d4 directly because of 3...Qh4† forcing the awkward 4.Ke2. After all, White did weaken the e1-h4 diagonal with his second move.

3. Nf3 ...

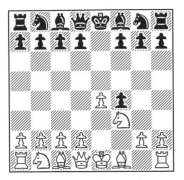

After the text move, ...Qh4† is prohibited and White can get on with his plan. Curiously, he could play 3.Bc4 (the Bishop's Gambit) allowing 3...Qh4† 4.Kf1 and then with Ng1-f3, try to demonstrate that Black's queen is misplaced.

3. ...   d5

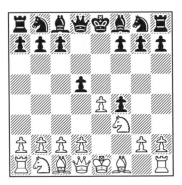

The all-purpose anti-gambit move. Take the pawn and then give it back is the motto for the defense. Other moves are possible, e.g. 3...g5, but then Black risks getting outgunned in the center, and if, in addition, he falls behind in development, he can get run over pretty quickly. That happens a lot in the King's Gambit.

4. exd5   ...

Black's counterattack in the center, threatening to take the e4-pawn, forces White to make an adjustment; he stops to take Black's queen pawn.

4. ...   Nf6

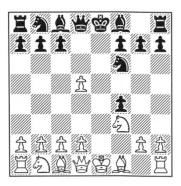

Setting up recapture with the knight. This is better than 4...Qxd5 when Black loses developing time to 5.Nc3, hitting the queen.

5. Nc3 ...

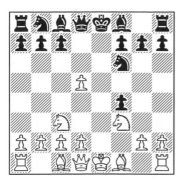

Alternatives are 5.c4 and 5.Bb5†. It's hard to say what's best.

5. ... Nxd5

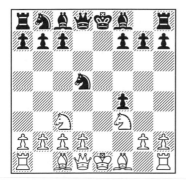

Black is still a pawn ahead, and White struggling to show compensation. If 6.Nxd5 Qxd5 7.d4 Be7! 8.Bxf4? then 8...Qe4† wins.

1. e4   ...

There's a sneaky way to get to the King's Gambit via Bird's Opening. It goes like this: 1.f4 (the Bird) 1... e5 (From's Gambit) 2.e4 Voilla! King's Gambit. But that's only if you're sneaky. In any case 1.e4 is an outstanding move no matter what opening you wish to play.

1. ...   e5

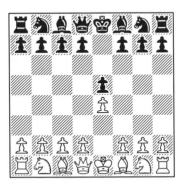

An excellent reply which, however, provides White with a target to attack.

2. f4   ...

Going after the center pawn with a flank pawn, a strategy that goes back to the very early days of chess. The strategy is still valid, but here in the King's Gambit, it is linked to a pawn sacrifice which may or may not be fully correct.

2. ...   Bc5

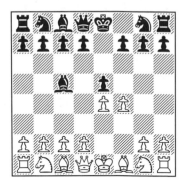

For psychological reasons Black declines the gambit. The idea of playing on the opponent's home court does not appeal. But positionally the move of the bishop is well founded. It develops a piece and strikes along the a7-g1 diagonal, weakened by the advance of the

82

f-pawn. Note that White cannot readily castle with the bishop at c5.

3. Nf3 ...

And not 3.fxe5? falling into Black's trap: 3...Qh4† and wins no matter what the reply. However, after the knight move, stopping ...Qh4† 4.fxe5 is once again on the agenda and Black must take note.

3. ... d6

Guards e5. On 4.fxe5 dxe5 5.Nxe5 Black has 5...Qh4† or even 5...Qd4.

4. Nc3 ...

Developing. The alternative is to put the pawn on c3 and then advance d2-d4.

4. ... Nf6

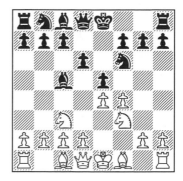

On 4...Nc6 Black has to contend with pinning 5.Bb5. The text is a semi-waiting move. After the bishop comes to c4 Black will bring his knight to c6 and if White then wants to pin, it will cost him a full tempo, Bc4-b5.

5. Bc4 ...

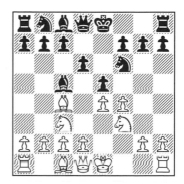

The bishop must come out and thanks to Black's fourth move finesse, there's no better square than c4, which admittedly, looks like a good post for the bishop. It is.

5. ...   Nc6

Consistent with Black's previous moves (1...e5, 2...Bc5, 3...d6) all of which form a strategy to control dark squares in the center (d4, e5). The likely follow up is 6.d3 Bg4.

23 King's Indian Attack

1. Nf3 ...

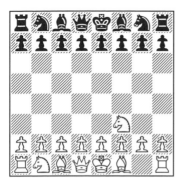

In the old days this was Zuckertort's Opening, and before that Irregular. Today 1.Nf3 is part of the Reti family because it was Richard Reti in the 1920s who first showed how the knight move can be woven into a system of its own.

1. ... d5

Black takes no particular notice of White's first move other than to see that 1...e5? 2.Nxe5 drops a pawn. Since he can't advance his e-pawn, he goes with his d-pawn. That's fair enough.

2. g3 ...

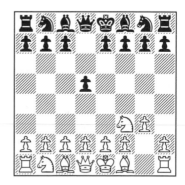

Reti liked 2.c4, a reverse Benoni but with an extra move for his side. The text heads for the King's Indian setup where White again has the extra move.

2. ...   Nf6

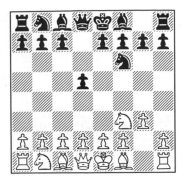

Black just develops. As is well known, developing moves are good for the player making them.

3. Bg2   ...

Finishing off the fianchetto begun with his last move.

3. ...   e6

Since the e-pawn cannot readily get to e5, Black settles for e6. His

main thought now is to get the f8-bishop out and then castle. It's a decent plan.

4. 0-0   ...

White constructs a domicile for his king: three pawns around the castled position, plus a bishop, a knight, and a rook. That's a lot of protection. At least the king will sleep at night.

4. ...   Be7

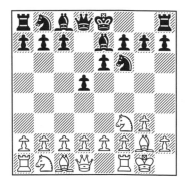

Black is also thinking about his king's security. He wants his bishop out so he too can castle.

5. d3   ...

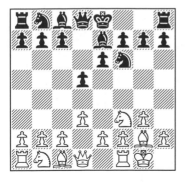

when the opposing pieces and pawns come into contact.

The placement of the White pawn at d3, rather than d4, is a characteristic move of the King's Indian Attack. White aims to post his queen-knight at d2 and then make his stand in the center, e2-e4, or perhaps a blow from the flank, c2-c4.

5. ...   0-0

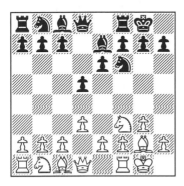

Black deems his position safe enough to castle. The game is just getting underway with chances even. It will get more interesting

24 King's Indian Defense

1. d4 ...

White stakes out territory in the center. If given the opportunity he'll take even more space by bringing his king pawn up to e4.

1. ... **Nf6**

So that if 2.e4? Nxe4.

2. c4 ...

White takes another track, advancing his c-pawn to control d5.

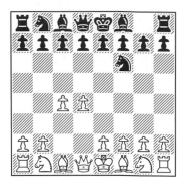

2. ... **g6**

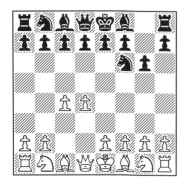

Black senses chances on the long dark-squared diagonal, and seeks to place his bishop in fianchetto at g7.

3. Nc3 ...

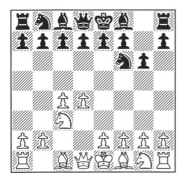

White develops his knight and strikes at the e4-square. That raises the question: Is Black willing to let White get in e2-e4?

3. ... Bg7

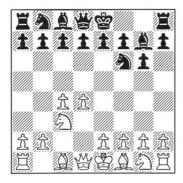

Black is not especially concerned. He's counting on his dark square control to keep White at bay. The alternative, if he wants to bail out, is the Grünfeld Defense, 3...d5.

4. e4 ...

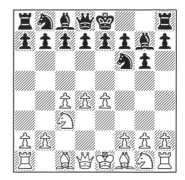

There are other moves, but when your opponent allows you to seize more center space, you should do it.

4. ... d6

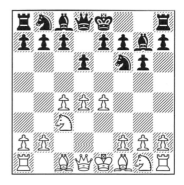

Hinders the advance 5.e5 now met by 5...dxe5 6.dxe5 Qxd1† 7.Kxd1 Ng4, and the White pawn is lost.

5. Nf3   ...

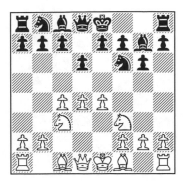

The Classical Variation with development of the White knight at f3. Alternatives are the Four Pawns Attack, 5.f2-f4, and the Sämisch Variation, 5.f2-f3. These lines are all good. Pick one and play it.

5. ...   0-0

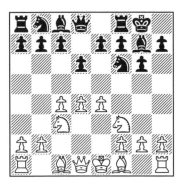

Black makes a safe haven for his king, come what may. On 6.Be2 he can hit the center with 6...c5 or perhaps 6...e5.

25 Larsen's Opening

1. b3

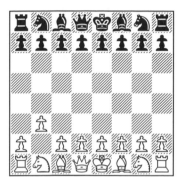

One of those offbeat flank openings whose immediate object is to make a place for the bishop at b2.

1. ... e5

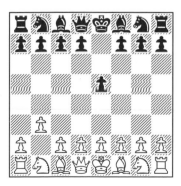

Black's aim is to support his e5-pawn blunting the effect of the enemy bishop when it comes to b2.

2. Bb2 ...

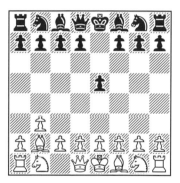

Having said "A," he pretty much has to continue with "B," else his first move makes no sense. From b2 the bishop strikes down the long diagonal and the immediate threat is to take the pawn at e5. How does Black defend the pawn?

2. ... f6

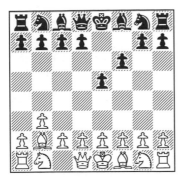

The most ambitious defense of the e5-pawn, more so than 2...d6. Using the f-pawn to guard e5, Black leaves his d-pawn free to advance to d5. That's the intention anyway.

3. e4 ...

The d5-square must be challenged before Black gets his pawn there. White can do it with his c-pawn (c2-c4) or with his e-pawn as in the text.

3. ... Bc5

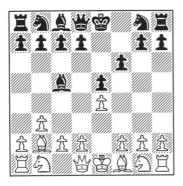

Seeing that 3...d5 is met by 4.exd5, Black foregoes any further pawn moves, and develops his bishop.

4. Bc4 ...

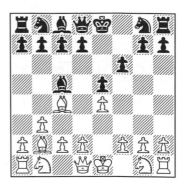

Threatens 5.Bxg8 Rxg8 6.Qh5† and 7.Qxh7.

4. ... Ne7

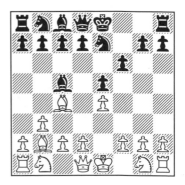

Black sidesteps the threat.

5. Qh5† ...

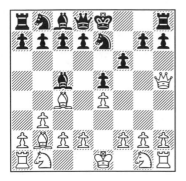

A probing check. Maybe Black will miss 5...Kf8?? 6.Qf7# Maybe he'll allow his knight to be pinned after 5...Ng6, or maybe he'll advance a pawn.

5. ...   g6

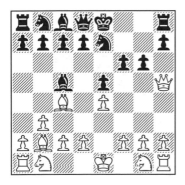

The g-pawn blocks the check and drives the queen from h5. Moving the pawn weakens Black's kingside pawn structure, but White loses time with his queen. So maybe things balance out. Then again, maybe they don't.

26 Latvian Gambit

1. e4 ...

Here the White pawn can become a target for attack since the square e4, upon which the pawn resides, is unguarded. But that fact alone should not deter White from making this strong central advance. Should Black later attack the pawn, White has the resources to deal with it when it occurs.

1. ... e5

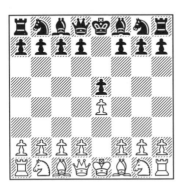

With this advance Black fixes the White e4-pawn in place so that it may not move forwards. That's rule number one when you're setting up

to attack some point in the enemy camp. Fix the target so it can't run away, then attack it.

2. Nf3 ...

It turns out that Black's e5-pawn is also fixed in place and subject to attack, here by the White knight coming to f3.

2. ... f5

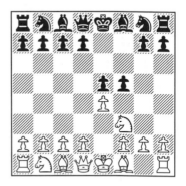

The characteristic move of the Latvian Gambit, really a counterattack on the e4-pawn. The notion is, you take my king pawn, then I take yours. In practice it's not quite as simple as that, but in any case that's the basic idea.

3. Nxe5 ...

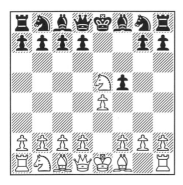

Capturing with the knight (instead of 3.exf5) opens the diagonal for 3.Qh5†. This would be the case if Black blindly played 3...fxe4?

3. ... Qf6

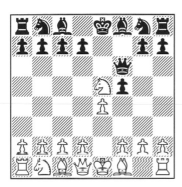

Attacks the knight. Black is prepared to meet 4.Qh5† with 4... g6 when both queen and knight are under threat of capture.

4. d4 ...

Also 4.Nc4, simply moving the knight out of danger. But White prefers to keep it guarded, holding c4 open for his bishop. With a knight on e5 and a bishop on c4 White can then threaten invasion at f7.

4. ... d6

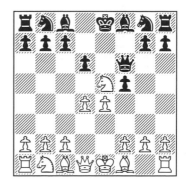

Chasing the enemy knight from Black's half of the board before it can do damage. Go away knight.

5. Nc4 ...

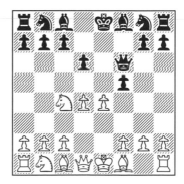

The knight finds sanctuary in his own half of the board. That's the safe half from White's perspective.

5. ...   fxe4

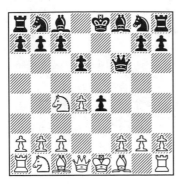

After a delay of two moves, while he attended to White's threats, Black at last is able to recover his gambit pawn. Material is once again even and the opening phase continues, each side having his chances. Although, White, by virtue of moving first, still has some initiative.

27 Modern Benoni Defense

1. d4	**...**	**2. c4**	**...**

Playing the d-pawn out early presents Black with a target which he can attack either from e5 or c5. All the same it should not deter White from playing d2-d4. If Black attacks it White should be able to deal with it one way or another.

1. ...   Nf6

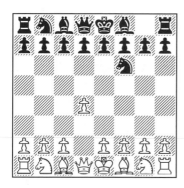

The Modern Benoni starts with the preliminary knight move to f6. The old version begins with an immediate advance of the Black pawn to c5, engaging d4.

Experience has shown that White's b1-knight coming to c3 works best when the pawn is placed at c4.

2. ...   c5

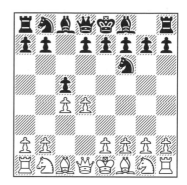

The characteristic move of the Benoni, really an attack from the flank on the d4-pawn.

3. d5   ...

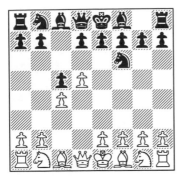

The strongest reply. White advances into enemy territory gathering space.

3. ...   e6

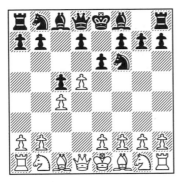

4. Nc3   ...

White develops and supports the d5-pawn. In addition the knight guards e4 and prepares for the advance of the e-pawn.

4. ...   exd5

Black continues his program, trading pawns at d5 and opening the king's file from his end of the board.

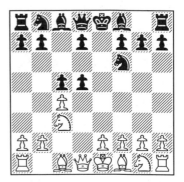

5. cxd5   ...

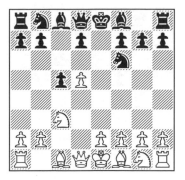

Recaptures with his pawn, keeping control of c6 and e6, two squares where Black could conceivably develop his pieces, ...Nc6 or ...Be6.

5. ...   d6

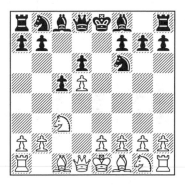

After White has pushed his pawn to d5 the long dark-squared diagonal is open for Black's bishop. On the agenda is ...g6 along with ...Bg7. Then comes Black castling and after that placing the rook at e8 to restrain the White e-pawn.

28 Nimzo-Indian Defense

1. d4 ...

Intending to form the ideal pawn center with 2.e2-e4.

1. ... Nf6

Prevents 2.e4. True 1...d5 does the job but the knight move is more flexible, keeping White guessing if d7-d5 will come or not.

2. c4 ...

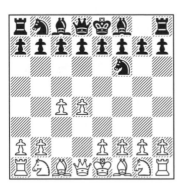

Pressure on d5 in case Black decides on d7-d5.

2. ... e6

Opens a path for the f8-bishop. Just where it will come out is not yet certain but could depend on White's next move.

3. Nc3 ...

Moving the knight to c3 White signals his intention to fight for control of the light center squares. Clearly he wants to get in e2-e4.

3. ... Bb4

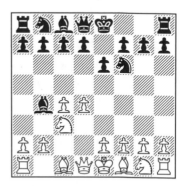

The characteristic move of the Nimzo-Indian. The bishop pins the knight and thereby prevents e2-e4. Black attempts to control the center square e4 with his pieces. Instead, 3...d5 transposes to the normal lines of the Queen's Gambit Declined.

4. Qc2   ...

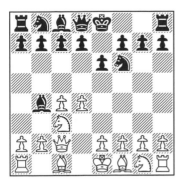

A dual purpose queen move. From c2 the queen observes the center square e4 and also from c2 she is prepared to answer ...Bxc3† with Qxc3, thereby avoiding doubled c-pawns. Alternatives to the queen move are many. In fact everything that is not too crazy has been seen, but nothing has yet been found to refute the Nimzo-Indian.

4. ...   d5

After White has moved his queen, the d1-pawn is momentarily undefended.

This prompts Black to show his cards and finally he does advance his queen pawn after all. The threat is 5...dxc4 and then 6...Qxd4. Other methods to attack d4 arise through 4...c5 or 4...Nc6. These are but two other variations in the Nimzo-Indian and there are plenty more which we cannot get into.

5. cxd5   ...

Deals with the threat to his c-pawn by exchanging it for the d5-pawn. This is why the pawn came to c4 in the first place.

5. ...   Qxd5

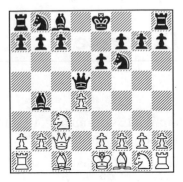

Of course 5...exd5 is steadier but somewhat more passive. With his queen capture Black intends to bring pressure to bear on the d4-pawn. Presumably White will defend with 6.e3 or 6.Nf3 and Black will hit back with 6...c5 along with ...Nc6.

29 Nimzovitch's Defense

1. e4   ...

The start of a space-gaining operation. Ideally White wants both his e and d pawns in the middle.

2. ...   Nc6

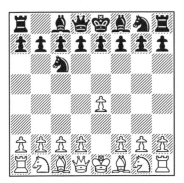

Nimzovitch's specialty. Black develops while striking at d4 and e5. Nevertheless, this move has never caught on because it allows White to achieve his mini goal.

2. d4   ...

White forms his pawn center. Black has to strike back quickly,

before White's command of central points becomes unshakable.

2. ...   d5

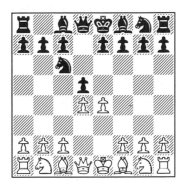

This is good. Black hits at the undefended e4-pawn forcing White to come to a decision.

3. e5   ...

White advances into Black territory, gaining ground as he does so, while taking control of f6.

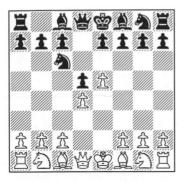

3. ...   Bf5

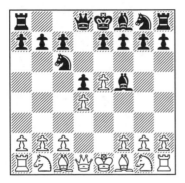

Since 3...f6 can be answered by 4.f4 giving support to the e5-pawn, Black forgoes further pawn moves in favor of developing his light-squared bishop.

4. c3   ...

Not falling for 4.Bd3? Nxd4 when Black gains a pawn. White, first of all, secures his d4-pawn. He also prevents ...Nb4, which could prove annoying.

4. ...   e6

Note the timing of Black's 3rd and 4th moves. Had Black played 3...e6, his light squared bishop would be locked in at c8.

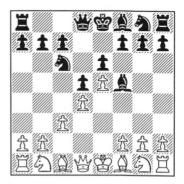

5. Ne2   ...

In order to attack the enemy bishop by playing the knight to g3. Note that White does not block his f-pawn with Nf3. He still intends to meet ...f7-f6 with f2-f4.

5. ...   Nge7

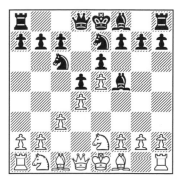

Black utilizes the vacant e7-square to bring out his kingside knight which would otherwise have trouble coming off the back rank. In the resulting position White has more space to maneuver while Black's game is fairly solid.

30 Old Indian Defense

1. d4 ...

With this push White indicates his desire to control the e5-square in Black's camp. Can he do it? It depends on how Black decides to arrange his center pawns.

1. ... Nf6

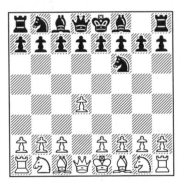

For the moment Black does not show his cards. The knight move is good and gives away nothing about how he will eventually set up his center pawns.

2. c4 ...

White continues forming his pawn center, the c-pawn striking at d5.

2. ... d6

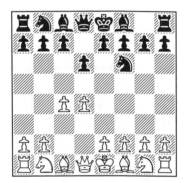

Aha!. Black reveals his plans. Playing his pawn to d6 (not 2... d5), Black shows that he intends to contest control of e5.

3. Nc3 ...

Or 3.Nf3 which temporarily holds up e7-e5. However, the b1-knight is destined for c3 since it is clearly the best square. The g1-knight has the option of f3 or e2, after the e-pawn has moved.

3 ...   e5

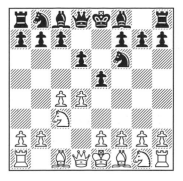

4. ...   Nbd7

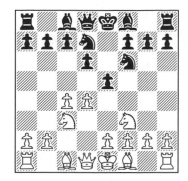

Black makes his play, challenging White for control of dark squared points in the middle. Black does not fear 4.dxe5 dxe5 5.Qxd8† Kxd8. He has ...c7-c6, then places his king at c7, where he's perfectly safe.

4. Nf3   ...

The knight declares for f3, supporting the pawn at d4, also threatening to take twice at e5.

White threatened to win the e5-pawn, so Black guards with his b8-knight. His strategy is to set up a strong point in the center at e5 which he hopes will keep White at bay. Note how the knight now blocks the c8-bishop. In the following play he has to be careful not to jam himself up much further.

5. e4   ...

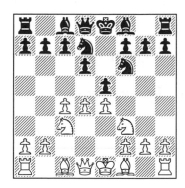

White advances his e-pawn to the center securing more space for his side. Other moves are 5.d5 or 5.dxe5. These are okay, but they release the tension in the center and make it easier for Black to play out his game. There's also 5.Bg5 as well as 5.g3 with 6.Bg2 and possible action down the long diagonal.

5. ...   Be7

Clearing out space between his king and rook; in short getting ready to castle. The modest placement of the bishop at e7, along with the pawn formation d6, e5, is typical of the Old Indian Defense. Black is solid but a bit cramped.

31 Owen's Defense

1. e4 ...

While 1.e4 is an excellent starting move, White must understand that's he's providing the opponent with a target, since e4, at the moment, is an undefended square in the center.

1. ... b6

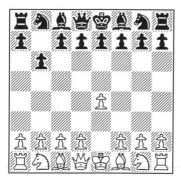

Preparing to lay siege to the e4-pawn by developing his queenside bishop in fianchetto. This move and his next one are the identifying moves of Owen's Defense.

2. d4 ...

At present nothing in White's camp is under attack so can use his turn to establish himself in the center. Two pawns side by side in the center (d4, e4) is one of the best openings a player can have.

2. ... Bb7

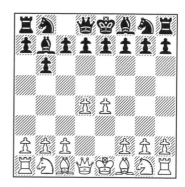

Having started the financhetto, Black is advised to complete it. From b7 the bishop bears down on e4 placing the pawn under fire. White may not ignore the attack as then Black captures an important pawn for free.

3. Bd3 ...

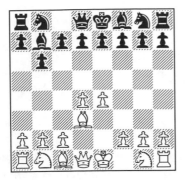

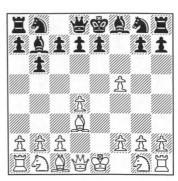

There are other ways to protect the e4-pawn (3.f3 and 3.Nc3 come to mind), but the bishop move appears the most natural. There is one caveat. In moving his bishop White leaves his g2-pawn undefended and this situation carries with it another set of responsibilities.

3. ...   f5?!

A consistent attack on e4, but all the same a risky adventure, in that Black weakens the h5-e8 diagonal leading to his king. Undoubtedly, the safer move is 3...e6.

4. exf5   ...

White accepts the offered pawn. It would appear that he's fallen into Black's trap, but in fact White has a trap of his own that he wants to spring.

4. ...   Bxg2

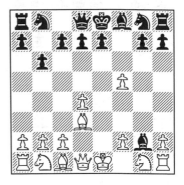

The bishop springs out of ambush. First the g2-pawn goes while next on the menu is the h1-rook.

5. Qh5†   ...

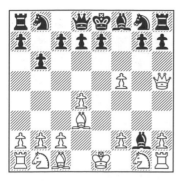

The queen pops out with check looking to exploit the weakness of the h5-e8 diagonal. The king cannot easily find shelter.

5. ...   g6

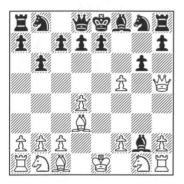

Black attempts to block the diagonal attack of the enemy forces. It's not clear that this can be done, for after 6.fxg6 Nf6 7.gxh7† Nxh5 8.Bg6 Black is mated. Instead, 6... Bg7 improves, but even in this case Black faces a formidable attack.

32 Petroff's Defense

1. e4 ...

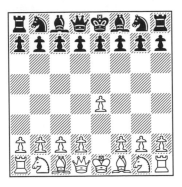

An invitation to symmetrical play should Black copy White's first move. But whether Black copies or not, 1.e4 is good, occupying and controlling center squares, and opening lines for development.

1. ... e5

Black copies. In itself this is not indicative of future symmetrical intentions. It's the next move that tells what Black is really up to.

2. Nf3 ...

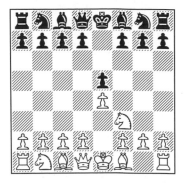

Attacking the e5-pawn. How will Black defend?

2. ... Nf6

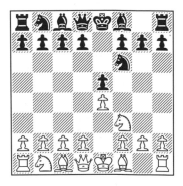

The copycat Petroff which is not really a defense at all, but a counter attack on the White e4-pawn.

3. Nxe5 ...

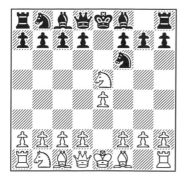

Accepting the challenge and at the same time setting a trap. Can Black afford to copy once again? The trap goes 3...Nxe4? 4.Qe2 Nf6 5.Nc6† winning the queen.

3. ... d6

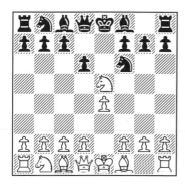

Before taking at e4 Black must first drive the e5-knight back to his own side of the board. That's the purpose of moving the pawn up to d6.

4. Nf3 ...

The frisky sac 4.Nxf7 is fun to play, especially in speed games. In slower games, the safe withdrawal to f3 is preferred.

4. ... Nxe4

If he doesn't take back he's lost a pawn for nothing, and that's not why people play the Petroff.

5. Qe2 ...

The alternative is 5.d4 d5 6.Bd3 and 7.0-0. With the queen move White pins the knight to the e-file; in fact he threatens to take it.

5. ... Qe7

If 5...d5 or 5...f5, then 6.d3 wins the pinned knight. But the queen move is quite a sufficient defense.

There follows

6. **d3**   **Nf6**
7. **Bg5**   **Qxe2†**
8. **Bxe2**   **Be7**

White enjoys a slight edge in the queenless middle-game. Exploiting it requires great stocks of patience.

33 Philidor's Defense

1. e4 ...

The main opening in Philidor's time (mid to late 1700s) and also in the following century as well.

1. ... e5

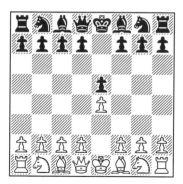

The standard response whereby Black plays for parity in the center.

2. Nf3 ...

An attack on e5 which Black is required to meet. How this plays out is up to Black, but he can't let the pawn go for nothing. That's bad play.

2. ... d6

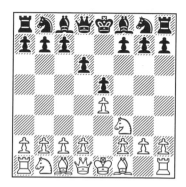

Philidor's recommendation, over the then-standard 2...Nc6. The idea is to provide solid protection to the e5-pawn, and there is nothing more solid than to guard a pawn with another pawn.

3. Bc4 ...

White develops his bishop and clears the decks for castling should the need arise. The alternative is the central strike 3.d4 upon which Philidor recommended the counter 3...f5.

3. ... Bg4

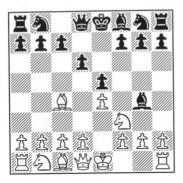

A byproduct of Black's second move, the bishop is released and pins the f3-knight. Idea: Knight moves, bishop takes queen.

4. Nc3 ...

White develops his queenside knight.

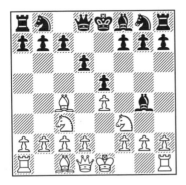

4. ... g6?

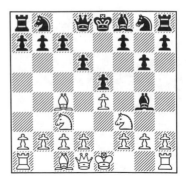

Hemmed in by the d6-pawn Black aims to bring his bishop to g7. The idea is not bad but first he should bring out a knight.

5. Nxe5! ...

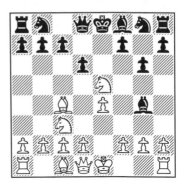

The pinned knight moves!

5. ... Bxd1?

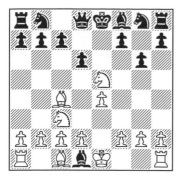

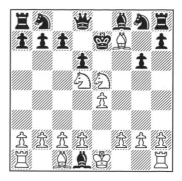

If 5...dxe5 then 6.Qxg4. But he's overlooked...

It seems that some pins are made to be broken. This is the famous Legal Mate and Black fell into it.

6. Bxf7† Ke7

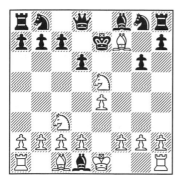

7. Nd5# 1-0

34 Pirc Defense

1. e4 ...

The most popular move, certainly at the amateur level. By moving out his king's pawn White gathers momentum for future operations.

1. ... d6

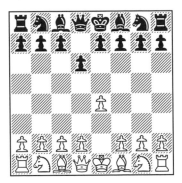

A quiet reply whereby Black restrains the further advance of White's e-pawn while opening a line for the eventual development of his light-squared bishop at c8.

2. d4 ...

When in doubt, put two pawns in the center. The White pawns at d4 and e4 control an entire block of squares, c5, d5, e5, f5. Black cannot place a piece on these squares without losing material.

The only way Black can contest this complex of center squares is with his pawns, and these have to be properly protected.

2. ... Nf6

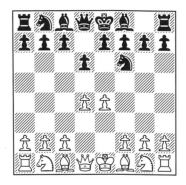

Developing with an attack on the e4-pawn. Beneath the surface Black also baits a trap. For if White rambunctiously advances his e-pawn, there comes: 3.e5 dxe5 4.dxe5 Qxd1† 5.Kxd1 Ng4, when

118

Black either wins the e5-pawn, or else his knight breaks in at f2, forking king and rook.

3. Nc3 ...

White calmly develops his queenside-knight and guards his pawn at e4. You can't ask for a better move.

3. ... g6

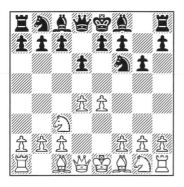

In conjunction with his first two moves, this is the characteristic move of the Pirc. Black prepares to fianchetto his dark-squared bishop at g7. He has other third moves but then it would not be a Pirc.

4.Nf3 ...

The most solid classical system of development. White's aim is to place knights on natural squares and get his king safely castled.

4. ... Bg7

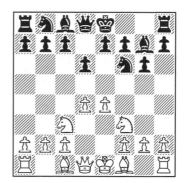

The bishop takes up its appointed post on the long dark-squared diagonal. Also, by clearing out space on his back rank, Black gets ready to castle.

5. Be2 ...

White anticipates ...Bg4 and breaks the pin in advance. On 5.Bc4 White has to be on the alert for the

"Fork Trick" 6...Nxe4, 7.Nxe4, d5, and there's still the matter of 5... Bg4.

5. ...   0-0

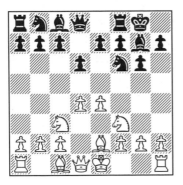

Before undertaking any action Black makes sure that his king is safely ensconced behind his castle walls.

35 Polish Opening

1. b4 ...

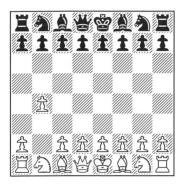

An offbeat flank opening with two ideas, (1) control the c5-square (2) develop the bishop at b2.

1. ... e5

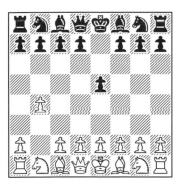

Naturally, Black has other first moves (...d5, ...Nf6) but the advance of the e-pawn threatens 2...Bxb4.

2. Bb2 ...

Proposing an exchange 2...Bxb4 3.Bxe5. In theory the trade of side pawn for center pawn should favor White, but in practice Black does okay. So 2...Bxb4 should not be dismissed out of hand. Also 2...d6 is quite reasonable.

2. ... f6

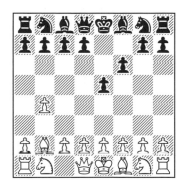

Black wants to do more than trade pawns; he wants to win a

pawn. So first he guards e5 after which he threatens to take on b4.

3. e4 ...

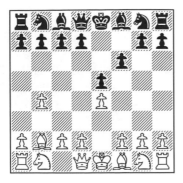

White switches gears, throwing caution to the wind while offering a gambit (which may or may not be correct). The safe way, if a bit pedestrian, was 3.a3 or 3.b5.

3. ... Bxb4

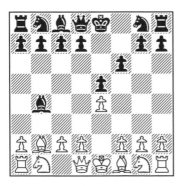

Black has no reason to turn down a free pawn so he takes, at the same

time developing his bishop and pinning the d2-pawn.

4. Bc4 ...

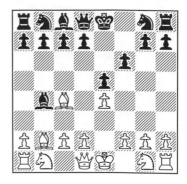

Threatening 5.Bxg8 Rxg8 6.Qh5† and 7.Qxh7.

4. ... Ne7

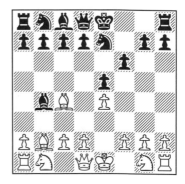

Black parries the threat by moving the knight off g8. From e7 the knight strikes at the center square d5.

5. f4 ...

White must continue in energetic fashion to break down the enemy center. Since the d2-pawn is pinned the choice falls on the f-pawn.

5. ... d5

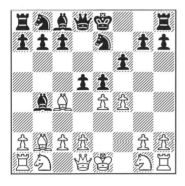

To close the diagonal of the c4-bishop. After 6.exd5 exf4 a lively game is in prospect; the onus is on White to justify his gambit.

36 Ponziani's Defense

1. e4 ...

In staking out his claim to the center White must understand that e4 is not a defended square and may well come under fire from enemy forces.

1. ... e5

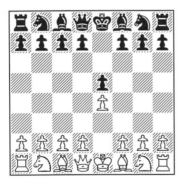

Black too must not become overconfident. The e5 square upon which he's just placed his pawn, is unguarded and subject to future attack.

2. Nf3 ...

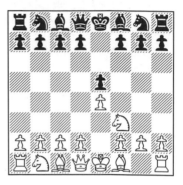

The future attack comes on the next move. The knight strikes e5 looking to take Black's pawn for nothing.

2. ... Nc6

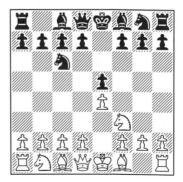

Black reacts by placing a knight guard on his e5-pawn. Clearly if White takes, 3.Nxe5? he comes up short after 3...Nxe5.

3. c3   ...

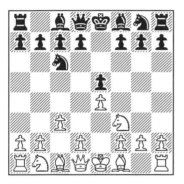

The characteristic move of the Ponziani. The pawn (not the knight) goes to c3 to take control of d4.

3. ...   Nf6

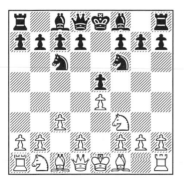

The fact that White cannot readily bring a knight to c3 is the signal for Black to attack the e4-pawn. Here he does it with his knight, but also the pawn moves, 3...d5 and 3...f5 can be tried as well.

4. d4   ...

White advances. On 4...exd4 comes 5.e5, and after the knight moves, 6.cxd4 recovering his pawn with control of the center.

4. ...   Nxe4

125

Removes the e4-pawn. Whatever happens afterwards, White will not wind up with two center pawns.

5. d5 ...

Drives the knight from c6, after which e5 is undefendable.

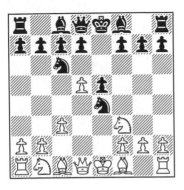

5. ... Nb8

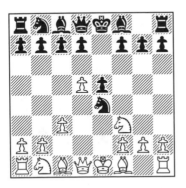

After ...d6, the knight can emerge at d7. The alternative was 5...Ne7 and then to g6. Of course, White soon recovers his pawn, Nxe5.

37 Queen's Gambit Accepted

1. d4 ...

One of the steadiest first moves White can play. The d4-pawn is guarded by the queen and cannot easily be shaken from its post.

1. ... **d5**

Black sets his pawn in the center. Whether he intends to keep it on d5 is another matter. We'll have to see from the subsequent play.

2. c4 ...

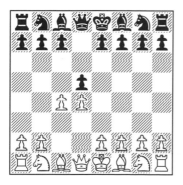

Pressure on d5 is best done by attacking it with another pawn. It has to be the c-pawn, for if 2.e4, Black takes, 2...dxe4, and enjoys an extra pawn.

2. ... **dxc4**

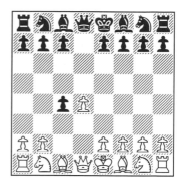

Goes back to the very early days when Black thought he was winning a pawn. We know that's not the case, but all the same, accepting the Queen's Gambit has survived to the 21st century.

3. e3 ...

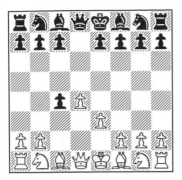

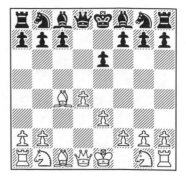

Probably White can get his pawn back immediately through 3.Qa4† and 4.Qxc4. That's why the Queen's Gambit is not a true gambit. But if he can land on c4 with his bishop, that's even better than bringing the queen out.

Develops his bishop and recovers the gambit pawn. The exchange at c4 has left White with two center pawns to Black's one. In the near future he may try to advance the e-pawn one more square.

4. ...   Nf6

3. ...   e6

On 3...b5, the undermining move 4.a4 insures that White gets his pawn back.

For example; 4...c6 5.axb5 cxb5 6.Qf3, winning material. When Black realized he couldn't keep the pawn he went over to normal moves.

4. Bxc4   ...

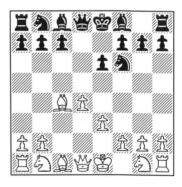

Black is alert and develops his kingside-knight taking command of the e4-square.

5. Nf3   ...

White also develops his kingside knight, clearing out space so that he's ready to castle.

5. ...   c5

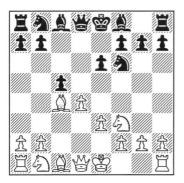

An attack on the d-pawn to keep White honest in the center. In the event of 6.dxc5 Black takes back with his bishop. He could first trade queens at d1. And if White castles, Black has the option of taking ...c5xd4, either now or later.

38 Queen's Gambit Albin Counter Gambit

1. d4 ...

The plan is to control the point e5, which means that if Black puts a pawn on this square White takes it.

1. ... d5

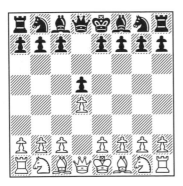

Think of this as fixing the target, blockading the d4-pawn so it cannot advance, and then later attacking it.

2. c4 ...

Continuing in normal fashion. He expects Black to take ...dxc4 or else guard the d5-pawn ...c6 or ...e6. He's in for a shock.

2. ... e5

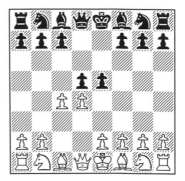

The Albin Counter Gambit. Black does nothing of the kind. Instead he goes straight for counterattack, looking to knock out White's d4-pawn.

3. dxe5 ...

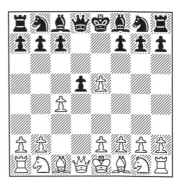

Following common sense principles, White takes the undefended pawn.

3. ...   d4

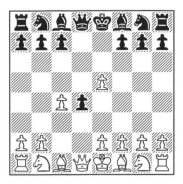

Black's idea. Having lured the d-pawn to e5, Black's queen pawn is able to advance into White's territory, gaining space, and hindering the natural development of the b1-knight to c3.

Unfortunately for White 4.e3? allows a beautiful trap with 4...Bb4†
5.Bd2 dxe3 6.Bxb4 exf2† 7.Ke2 fxg1/N†! and Black wins.

4. Nf3   ...

Hence White forgoes 4.e3 in favor of the g1-knight attacking the d4-pawn.

4. ...   Nc6

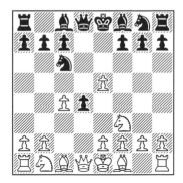

Develops the knight and defends his attacked pawn.

5. a3   ...

There are other moves, 5.Nbd2 or 5.g3, but all the same it is useful for White to control b4, preventing

Black from playing either his knight
or bishop there.

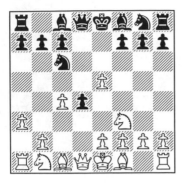

5. ...   a5

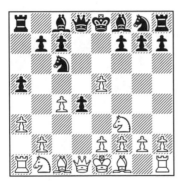

Keeps a lid on, stopping b2-b4.
Shortly, Black will post his bishop at
c5, over-protecting his d4-pawn.

39 Queen's Gambit Orthodox Defense

1. d4   ...

Occupies a center square (d4), controls another (e5), and opens a diagonal for the c1-bishop to come out. You can't ask more from an opening move.

1. ...   d5

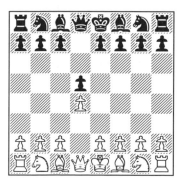

Black copies White's first move, maintaining symmetry. The effects, however, are slightly different. Whereas White's d4 seeks control of dark squares, Black's ...d5 aims at controlling light squares.

2. c4   ...

Played to lure the d5-pawn out of the center, ...dxc4, which would then leave White with two center pawns, d and e, versus Black's one center pawn, the e-pawn.

2. ...   e6

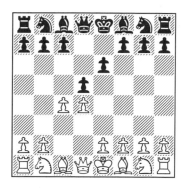

Black guards his d5-pawn with another pawn. If now 3.cxd5, then 3...exd5 keeping his grip on the central light squares.

3. Nc3   ...

In the Queens Gambit, White develops his b1-knight only after his pawn has jumped out to c4. The two moves are consistent and mutually supporting. They both add to the pressure White is exerting on the enemy d5-pawn.

3. ... Nf6

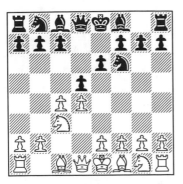

Black develops his kingside knight with a view to countering the pressure of the opposing c3-knight. From f6, the Black knight controls d5 as well as e4.

4. Bg5 ...

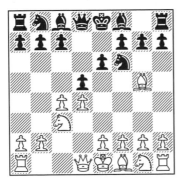

Excellent. White develops and pins the knight. The idea is 5.Bxf6 Qxf6 6.cxd5 exd5 7.Nxd5 gaining a pawn. Black would therefore have to recapture 5...gxf6, doubling f-pawns, and weakening his kingside.

4. ... Nbd7

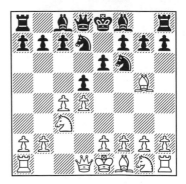

Ready to answer 5.Bxf6 with 5...Nxf6. Black lays a trap. The trap springs on 5.cxd5 exd5 6.Nxd5? Black ignores the pin 6...Nxd5! 7.Bxd8 Bb4† regaining his queen and emerging a piece ahead.

5. e3 ...

Playing 5.e3 White sidesteps the trap and gets on with rational development.

5. ...   **Be7**

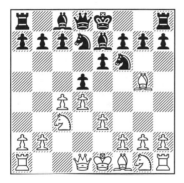

White avoided the pitfall, but there's no harm to Black's game. He unpins his knight, and gets ready to castle.

40 Queen's Gambit Slav Defense

1. d4 ...

White stakes out his claim for territory in the center.

2. ... d5

Black counters with his own claim, ramming up against the enemy d-pawn.

2. c4 ...

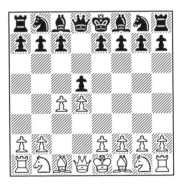

To lure Black's pawn out of the center, offering c4 as bait. Both understand that on 2...dxc4, White is sure to regain his pawn, with prospects of initiative.

2. ... c6

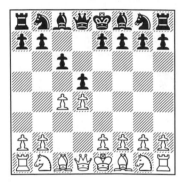

The Slav Defense. Black is content to guard d5 with his c-pawn. The advantage of ...c6 over ...e6, is that the light-squared c8-bishop has a diagonal to come out on. The disadvantage is that if Black changes strategy and later decides to attack White's center with his c-pawn, (c6-c5), it costs him a tempo.

3. Nf3 ...

There's no threat with this move. It's a combination developing move and waiting move. White wants to see just how Black intends to bring out his forces. And he deliberately leaves his c4-pawn without an obvious defense, still hoping to induce ...dxc4.

3. ...   Nf6

For the moment Black too is content to bring out a new piece. In the event that White relieves tension in the center with 4.cxd5, Black answers 4...cxd5, maintaining parity.

4. Nc3   ...

The knight moves into position attacking d5. Now 4...Bf5 is thought premature because of 5.cxd5 cxd5 6.Qb3, once again attacking d5, plus the newly undefended pawn at b7.

4. ...   dxc4

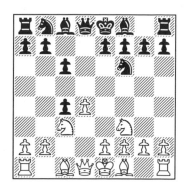

Black takes. White gets the pawn back in a couple of moves; meanwhile Black brings out his bishop.

5. a4   ...

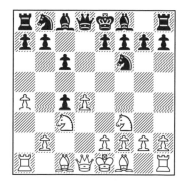

White takes time out to prevent
...b7-b5 so Black cannot support
the pawn at c4.

5. ...   Bf5

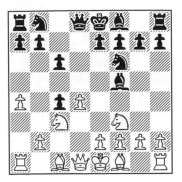

Black develops his bishop to the
center. With no d5-pawn on the
board, the f5-bishop and f6-knight
take up the function of controlling
e4. White will now try to get his
pawn back, either through 6.Ne5
and Nxc4 or by 6.e3 and Bxc4.

41 Queen's Gambit Tarrasch Defense

1. d4   ...

The double advance of the d-pawn announces White's presence in the center; and left alone e4 may follow.

1. ...   d5

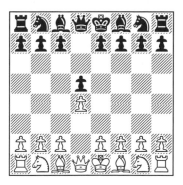

With his pawn at d5, Black is ready to answer 2.e4 with 2...dxe4.

2. c4   ...

An attack on the d5-pawn by the queen's bishop pawn; a flank attack if you will. If Black gets sidetracked, 2...dxc4, White may advance e2-e4.

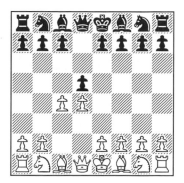

2. ...   e6

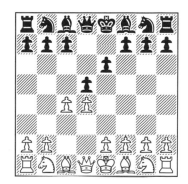

Pawn support. Black has no fear of an exchange as he replaces his d5-pawn with his e6-pawn, still maintaining control of e4.

3. Nc3 ...

There's no doubt that the b1-knight performs best on the c3-square where it pressures the d5-pawn.

3. ... c5

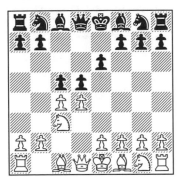

Tarrasch's move, designed to place White's d4-pawn under corresponding counter pressure. The thought is to induce e2-e3, guarding the pawn, but at the same time hemming in the c1-bishop.

4. cxd5 ...

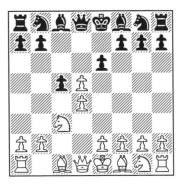

Capturing at d5 relieves some of the central tension. Also, he wants to see which pawn Black will take, the one on d5 or the other on d4.

4. ... exd5

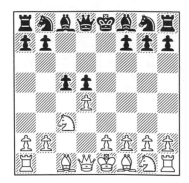

Recapture on d5 is best. Instead, 4...cxd4 5.Qxd4 Nc6 is the risky (unsound?) von Hennig-Schara gambit. For the pawn given up, Black hopes to obtain a lead in development.

5. Nf3 ...

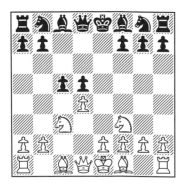

White holds off on e2-e3 and defends d4 with his knight. He's hoping to play Bc1-g5 with effect. This would happen if Black carelessly plays 5...Nf6.

5.   ...   Nc6

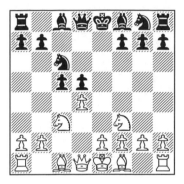

The correct knight. True, even after 5...Nc6. White can try 6.Bg5, but 6...Be7 is a sufficient answer.

42 Queen's Indian Defense

1. d4 ...

All you have to know is that 1.d4 puts a pawn in the center and it's a good way to begin a chess game.

1. ... **Nf6**

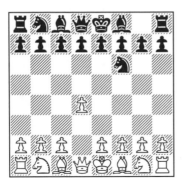

And you know you want to bring your pieces out so they control their fair share of the center squares. 1...Nf6 takes command of the points d5 and e4.

2. c4 ...

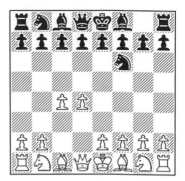

The chief merit of 2.c4 is that it sets up for battle in the center, fighting for control of the d5-square.

2. ... **e6**

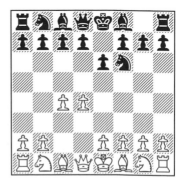

Defends d5. A good move.

3. Nf3 ...

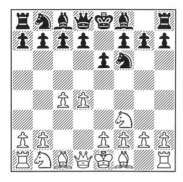

Develops a knight. Also good.

3. ... b6

The fiancehetto of the queen's bishop is the characteristic move of the Queen's Indian Defense. Black intends to brings his bishop to b7, where in conjunction with his f6-knight, it bears down on the important e4-square.

4. g3 ...

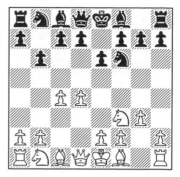

In order to counter the influence of Black's bishop on the long diagonal, White prepares to fianchetto his own light square bishop.

4. ... Bb7

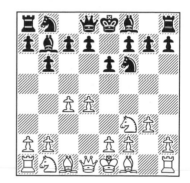

Black completes the fianchetto of his bishop.

5. Bg2 ...

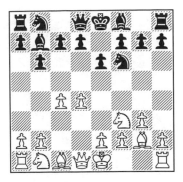

White does likewise. Now both sides have bishops on the long diagonal. After White castles he'll have one slight tactical advantage: his g2-bishop will be protected by his king, while the b7 bishop will remain unguarded.

5. ...   Be7

Black gets his bishop to the modest e7 square. Next turn he will use to get his king safely castled. Tough, grinding play lies ahead.

43 Ruy Lopez

1. e4 ...

Just before 1500, the rules changed and pawns were allowed to move out two "boxes." Before that it was only one "box." Legend has it that the first pawn ever to advance two squares was the king's pawn, today's e-pawn. Whether you believe the legend or not, the move of the e-pawn is just as good now as it was back in the time of Columbus.

1. ... e5

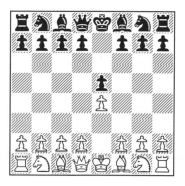

The e7-pawn flexes its muscles and likewise advances two boxes.

2. Nf3 ...

An attack on the Black e5-pawn. This signals White's main strategy in the Lopez.

2. ... Nc6

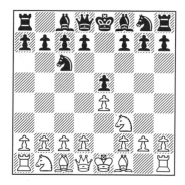

The pawn acquires a guardian in the form of Black's queen knight. It will be attacked next move.

3. Bb5 ...

The characteristic move of the Ruy Lopez. The bishop attacks the knight which guards e5. Is it a threat to win the e5-pawn or not?

3. ...   a6

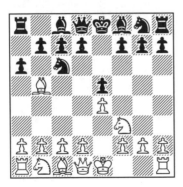

The answer is not yet. Black has time to attack and chase the bishop. Yes there are other third moves but they all seem to work a bit better when ...a6 is thrown in. So we throw it in.

4. Ba4   ...

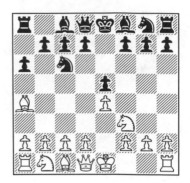

White could take the knight, 4.Bxc6 dxc6, and then the pawn, 5.Nxe5. But he can't hold on to it because of the queen fork at d4. So White backs the bishop off for the time being.

4. ...   Nf6

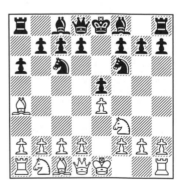

Black develops his knight with attack on the e4-pawn. How does White deal with it?

5. 0-0   ...

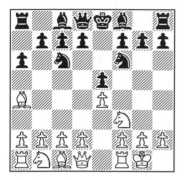

White could have defended by 5.Nc3 or 5.d3 but he allows Black to take, banking on getting it back, hopefully with interest.

5. ...   Nxe4

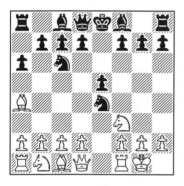

If he wanted to play it safe then 5...Be7 was available, getting ready to castle. But Black fears no evil and takes the pawn, opening up the game. The likely follow up is 6.d4 b5 7.Bb3 d5 8.dxe5 when White does indeed conquer e5, at the expense of e4.

44 Saragossa Opening

1. c3   ...

The Saragossa opening has little independent value since play usually transposes to something else.

1. ...   e5

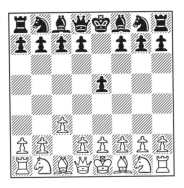

Since White threatens nothing Black has a wide choice of first moves. Advancing one of the pawns to the center (e5 or d5) cannot be bad.

2. d4   ...

At some point White has to make a stand in the center so he might as well do it now. 2.e4 was another possibility, but the text threatens to win a pawn.

2. ...   exd4

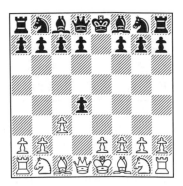

Black must react or he drops a pawn. Exchanging is as good as anything else.

3. cxd4   ...

White gets good value from his first move. The c-pawn comes to the center and c3 is vacated for the knight. Can one ask for more?

3. ...   d5

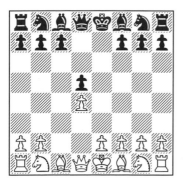

Black's e-pawn has been knocked out of commission so he makes his stand in the center with his d-pawn.

4. Nc3   ...

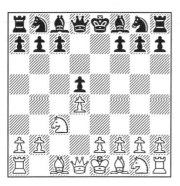

The queenside-knight comes out to an effective post, pressuring d5 and e4.

4. ...   Nf6

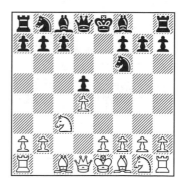

Reinforcing d5 and e4.

5. Bg5   ...

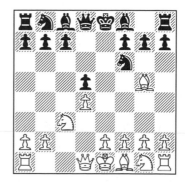

Threatens to break up Black's pawns by 6.Bxf6 gxf6 (not 6...Qxf6 7.Nxd5).

analysis after 6...gxf6

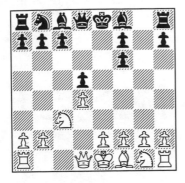

5. ...   Be7

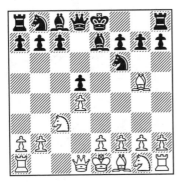

The play of the bishop neutralizes the pin, and in the event of Bg5xf6 Black is ready to recapture Be7xf6, keeping his pawn structure intact.

The astute openings expert will by now have recognized the sleight of hand transposition from the Saragossa Opening to the Exchange Variation of the Queen's Gambit Declined: 1.d4 d5 2.c4 e6 3.cxd5 exd5 4.Nc3 Nf6 5.Bg5 Be7. The same position.

45 Scotch Game

1. e4 ...

The start of a race to gain ground in the center. White, by virtue of his first move, has a slight advantage.

1. ... e5

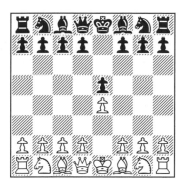

Black establishes his base of operations in the middle.

2. Nf3 ...

The e5 pawn provides a target and White goes after it. He now has one piece more in the field than Black.

2. ... Nc6

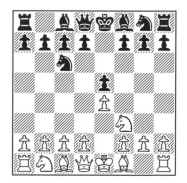

Black keeps up the pace, developing his queenside knight while defending his base at e5.

3. d4 ...

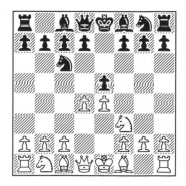

This pawn advance is the characteristic move of the Scotch and forces the issue. Besides adding another attacker to e5, White opens lines of development for his pieces. A good move serves multiple purposes.

3. ...   exd4

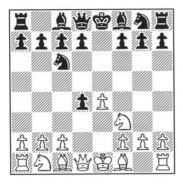

The e5-pawn gives way under the pressure and to avoid being lost, exchanges itself for the d4-pawn.

4. Nxd4   ...

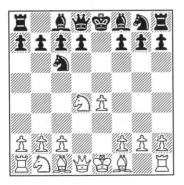

White recaptures at d4 which undoubtedly is his safest course. If he's feeling frisky he can offer a gambit either with 4.Bc4 or 4.c3.

4. ...   Bc5

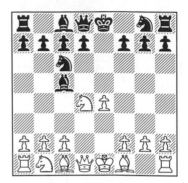

Black concentrates on getting his pieces out while challenging White in the center. At the moment he threatens to take twice at d4 winning a full piece.

5. Be3   ...

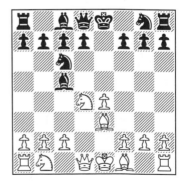

White defends knight with bishop, in turn threatening to win a piece by 6.Nxc6 bxc6 7.Bxc5.

5. ...   Bb6

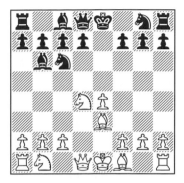

Placing the bishop on a protected square obviates the threat. If he didn't want to play the bishop, then the alternative was 5...Qf6, but that's a bit more complicated.

the alternative 5...Qf6

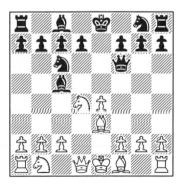

 46 Sicilian Defense

1. e4 ...

When White is feeling aggressive and plays to win, he usually starts by advancing 1.e2-e4. That's what Bobby Fischer used to do when he was White.

1. ... c5

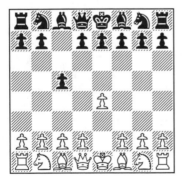

And when Black plays to win it's a good idea to try and unbalance the game by using the Sicilian Defense. That's what Bobby Fischer used to do when he was Black.

2. Nf3 ...

White aims to advance his pawn to d4 but if he does it immediately Black takes and then gains time on the White queen, for example 2.d4 cxd4 3.Qxd4 Nc6. That's why White brings his knight out—to take back on d4 with the knight.

2. ... Nc6

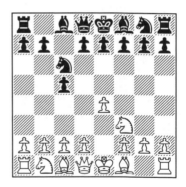

One of several 2nd moves Black can play: 2...d6 is one, 2...e6 is another. Often these transpose into the same position but also they can lead to systems that are quite independent.

3. d4 ...

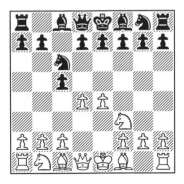

Playing for control of the center White forces his pawn to d4, opening the position. Note that the threat is not d4xc5 but d4-d5, driving on the knight.

3. ... cxd4

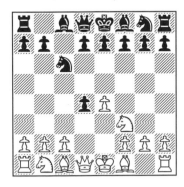

The reason for Black's first move. If a White pawn shows up at d4 he takes it.

White must not be allowed two pawns side by side in the center. That's the first idea of the Sicilian. Other ideas come later.

4. Nxd4 ...

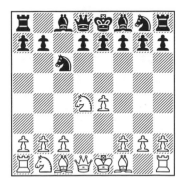

White recaptures the pawn with his knight. This was programmed into White's second move.

4. ... Nf6

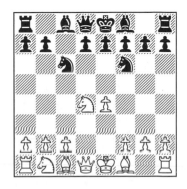

Develops his g8-knight and attacks the undefended e4-pawn.

Pressure on e4 is another typical Sicilian idea, perhaps the second idea, but they don't always tell you that.

5. Nc3   ...

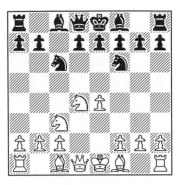

Develops and defends e4.

5. ...   d6

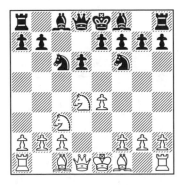

Or 5...e5, 5...e6. Sicilians can go in so many directions it's hard to keep track of all the theory. Some say that's why Bobby Fischer retired from the game.

47 Stonewall Attack

1. d4   ...

In the Stonewall Attack White plays for control of e5, a central square in the enemy camp. The d-pawn advance starts things off.

1. ...   d5

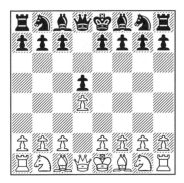

If Black could read minds he might play ...d6 throwing White off his game. But it's impossible to tell from one move what the opponent has planned. A good opening is flexible and can go in different directions.

2. e3   ...

In order to bring out the f1-bishop. In a number of these queen pawn games White emphasizes development of his kingside pieces, leaving some of his queenside forces, like the c1-bishop, sitting on their starting squares for a time.

2. ...   Nf6

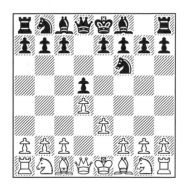

Black brings out his g8-knight to where it exerts its influence over the center squares d5 and e4.

3. Bd3   ...

Consistent with his previous move, White develops his bishop to its optimal post d3, striking through the central point e4, down the diagonal to h7, where he expects Black to place his king after castling.

3. ...   c5

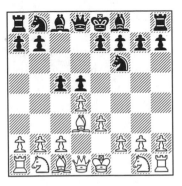

An attack by Black's queen bishop pawn on White's central strong point d4. There's another idea as well involving the further advance of the c-pawn to displace White's d3-bishop. Also, in the event White captures 4.dxc5, Black has various ways to get his pawn back, so that's not a big concern.

4. c3   ...

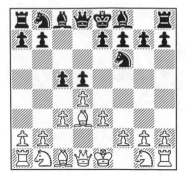

Not so much to guard d4, that's being done by the e3-pawn, but to make a space for the d3-bishop in case Black plays his pawn to c4. The reply is Bd3-c2.

4. ...   e6

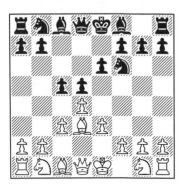

Opens a line for the f8-bishop and guards his c5-pawn. That's in case White decides to take on c5 and then support with b2-b4.

5. f4   ...

158

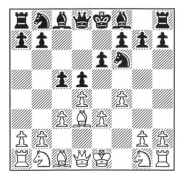

The characteristic move of the Stonewall Attack. White now has two of his pawns, the d- and f-pawns, lined up against the e5-square. The idea is to follow up with Ng1-f3 and then put the knight on e5.

5. ...   Nc6

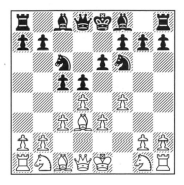

Black brings out his queenside knight to where it exercises some influence over e5. A possible alternative is 5...Ne4 (before White plays Nb1-d2) followed by 6...f5, a double Stonewall.

48 Three Knights' Game

1. e4 ...

White's bid for advantage in the center. It also opens lines for the queen and bishop, so it has several functions.

1. ... e5

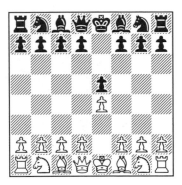

Also with multiple functions. It fixes e4 so it can't advance, controls dark squares (d4/f4) in the center, and clears space so the king, queen, and f8-bishop can now move around.

2. Nf3 ...

An attack on e5. That'll teach him to put a pawn in the center. Now he's got to be careful lest it gets lost.

2. ... Nc6

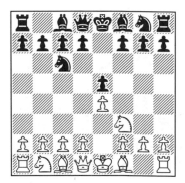

Black carefully guards his e5-pawn. When you place a pawn in the center you have an obligation to keep watch over it. That's all Black does here.

3. Nc3 ...

Giving preference to the knight over the f1-bishop.

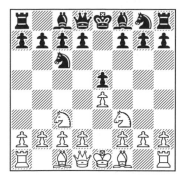

White follows the rules for developing his game and brings his knight towards the center. Notice how the White knights have encompassed all four center squares in their radius of attack (d4, e4, d5, e5).

3. ...   Bc5

Black could keep up the symmetry by playing Ng8-f6, the Four Knights' Game. But here there are only three knights in the field so that's how the opening gets its name.

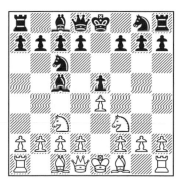

4. Nxe5   ...

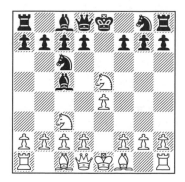

At first glance this looks like loss of a knight but it's not. In fact White has seen a tactic and figures he can safely take the e5-pawn.

4. ...   Nxe5

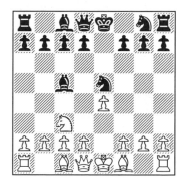

Or 4...Bxf2† 5.Kxf2 Nxe5. But after 6.d4, White with two pawns in the center, holds positional advantage.

5. d4   ...

161

has an edge as Black has no pawn in the center.

The fork part of the fork trick. This double attack on the enemy bishop and knight insures that While will recover his temporarily sacrificed piece.

5. ...   Bd6

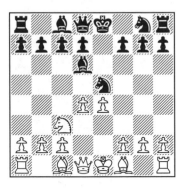

Black has to return the piece and looks to regain his pawn in the process. One way is 5...Bxd4 but it brings White's queen into action, 6.Qxd4. Thus a retreat with the follow up 6.dxe5 Bxe5. Still, White

49 Two Knights' Defense

1. e4 ...

One of the best ways to start a chess game.

1. ... e5

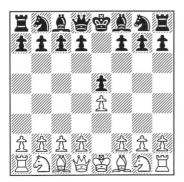

Both sides establish themselves in the center, opening lines for their respective kingside bishops.

2. Nf3 ...

White develops his knight and attacks the e5-pawn.

2. ... Nc6

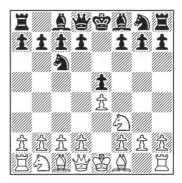

Black develops while placing a guard on the pawn, thereby neutralizing White's knight.

3. Bc4 ...

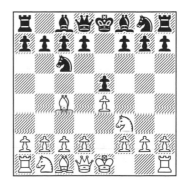

163

The bishop comes into the game courtesy of the White e-pawn which cleared the path. The bishop joins with the pawn to set up control over d5, all the while aiming at the f7-pawn.

3. ... Nf6

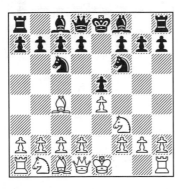

The g8-knight enters into action, attacking the e4-pawn. The drawback is that it blocks the path of the queen to g5, where White can place his knight.

4. Ng5 ...

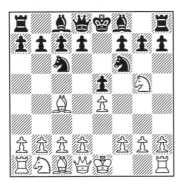

Since g5 is available, the knight moves into Black territory in order to combine with the c4-bishop in threatening f7.

4. ... d5

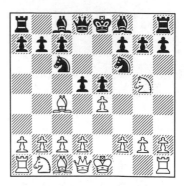

There is no way to get another defender on f7, so Black has to think creatively. The d-pawn cuts the line of the c4-bishop so f7 is safe.

5. exd5 ...

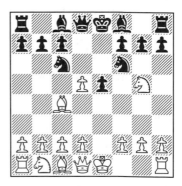

White is not going to allow d5xc4. The simplest plan is to capture d5

and attack the knight. The natural recapture 5...Nxd5 is deemed too risky after 6.Nxf7 Kxf7 7.Qf3†, the Fried Liver Attack. So something else is needed.

5.   ...   Na5

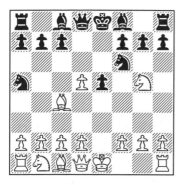

Sacrificing to chase the c4-bishop from the diagonal leading to f7. What follows? Probably 6.Bb5† c6 7.dxc6 bxc6 8.Be2 h6 9.Nf3 e4, and Black has an initiative for the pawn.

50 Van't Kruys Opening

1. e3 ...

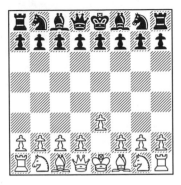

Van't Kruys Opening. Most often it transposes into something more recognizable later on.

1. ... e5

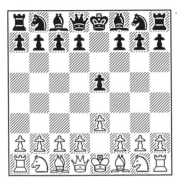

This two step advance carries more weight than White's one step push; it controls more space.

2. d4 ...

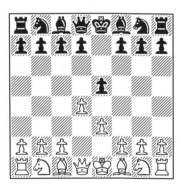

Tackles the e5-pawn, neutralizing it by exchange or else drawing it forward.

2. ...   exd4

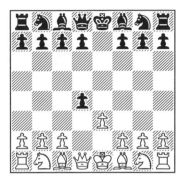

Rejecting e5-e4 as it will be difficult to support the pawn. The exchange at d4 is an even trade. Nobody gains, nobody loses.

3. exd4   ...

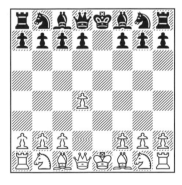

Replacing his pawn in mid-board. Inferior was 3.Qxd4 when 3...Nc6 chases the queen with loss of time.

3. ...   d5

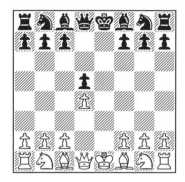

Black needs an outlet for his light squared bishop.

4. Nf3   ...

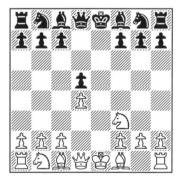

With the e-file open both sides should aim to castle as quickly as possible.

4. ...   Nf6

In the old days computers played 4...Qe7† which is not so good. White answers 5.Be2, 6.0-0, and 7.Re1.

5. Bd3   ...

Developing his kingside, getting ready to castle. Possible but passive is 5.Be2, while 5.Bb5† is a waste of time after 5...c6.

5 ...   Bd6

Completes the transposition from Van't Kruys to the exchange variation of the French Defense. The position normally comes about by 1.e4 e6 2.d4 d5 3.exd5 exd5 4.Nf3 Nf6 5.Bd3 Bd6. Figure on both sides now castling and then the development of the queenside forces.

51 Vienna Game

1. e4 ...

The starting move of many a chess game. The idea is to open pathways for queen and bishop to come into the game.

1. ... e5

Black answers in kind. For a brief moment, symmetry reigns on the board.

2. Nc3 ...

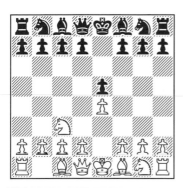

Vienna Game. The queen knight comes out observing the central points e4, d5, but otherwise the move threatens nothing.

2. ... Nf6

Since nothing is endangered Black has a free hand in his choice of replies. The development of the g8-knight tends to be the most popular but also seen are 2...Nc6 and even 2...Bc5.

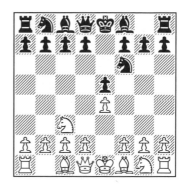

3. Bc4 ...

One of the main branches. The other is 3.f4, a cousin to the King's Gambit.

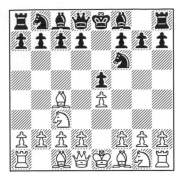

The bishop aims to control d5 in conjunction with the c3-knight and e4-pawn. Plus it eyes f7 where an attack may shortly take place.

3. ...   Nxe4

The fork trick. Neither 4.Bxf7† nor 4.Nxe4 d5 are dangerous for Black. White looks around and finds something else, a nasty queen move.

analysis: after 4.Nxe4 d5

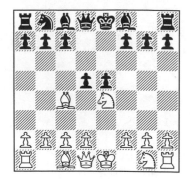

4. Qh5   ...

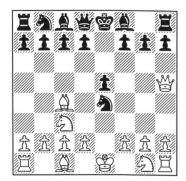

Mate threat at f7. That surely spells trouble along with threats to the e4-knight and e5-pawn.

4. ...   Nd6

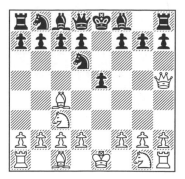 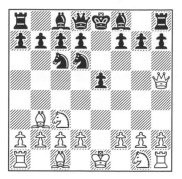

The best defense. The knight retreats to safety while covering the f7-mate threat. Also there's an attack on the c4-bishop.

5. Bb3   ...

White is ready to gambit a pawn to preserve his attacking bishop at c4. He can recover his pawn with 5.Qxe5† and then save his bishop. But Black has 5...Qe7 trading queens, killing off any attack. Apparently that line of play is too dull for White's taste.

5. ...   Nc6

Protects e5. After 6.Nb5 attacking the knight that guards the mate, the ball is in Black's court. In place of 5...Nc6 Black could let the e-pawn go and try 5...Be7 getting ready to castle. This is probably his safest play.

# Schematic Overview of the Openings

Double King Pawn Openings: 1.e4 e5
2.Bc4	Bishop's Opening
2.Nc3	Vienna Game
2.f4 exf4	King's Gambit Accepted
2.f4 Bc5	King's Gambit Declined
2.d4 exd4 3.Qxd4	Center Game
2.d4 exd4 3.c3	Danish Gambit

The King's Knight Opening: 1.e4 e5 2.Nf3
2...d6	Philidor Defense
2...Nf6	Petroff Defense
2...f5	Latvian Counter Gambit

1.e4 e5 2.Nf3 Nc6
3.c3	Ponziani Opening
3.d4	Scotch Game
3.Bb5	Ruy Lopez
3.Nc3 Bc5	Three Knights' Game
3.Nc3 Nf6	Four Knights' Game
3.Bc4 Nf6	Two Knights' Defense
3.Bc4 Be7	Hungarian Defense
3.Bc4 Bc5	Giuoco Piano
3.Bc4 Bc5 4.b4	Evans Gambit

Asymmetrical King Pawn: 1.e4
1...b6	Owen's Defense
1...c6	Caro-Kann Defense
1...c5	Sicilian Defense

1...e6	French Defense
1...d5	Center Counter Defense
1...d6	Pirc Defense
1...Nf6	Alekhine Defense
1...Nc6	Nimzovitch's Defense

Double Queen Pawn Openings: 1.d4 d5

2.Nf3 Nf6 3.e3	Colle System
2.e3 Nf6 3.f4	Stonewall Attack

Queens Gambit (Accepted and Declined):
1.d4 d5 2.c4

2...dxc4	Queen's Gambit Accepted
2...e5	Albin Counter Gambit
2...c6	QGD Slav Defense
2...e6	QGD Orthodox Defense
2...e6 3.Nc3 c5	QGD Tarrasch Defense

Asymmetrical   Q-Pawn 1.d4

1...f5	Dutch Defense

Indian Defenses: 1.d4 Nf6 2.c4

2...e5	Budapest Counter Gambit
2...d6	Old Indian Defense
2...c5 3.d5 b5	Benko Gambit
2...c5 3.d5 e6	Modern Benoni Defense
2...e6 3.Nf3 Bb4†	Bogoljubov Defense
2...e6 3.Nf3 b6	Queen's Indian Defense
2...e6 3.Nc3 Bb4	Nimzo-Indian Defense
2...g6 3.Nc3 d5	Grünfeld Defense
2...g6 3.Nc3 Bg7	King's Indian Defense

Flank and Unusual Openings

1.b3	Larsen's Opening
1.b4	Polish Opening

1.c4	English Opening
1.c3	Saragossa Opening
1.e3	Van't Kruys Opening
1.f4	Bird Opening
1.Nc3	Dunst Opening
1.Nf3 d5 2.g3	King's Indian Attack

FREE!
Poker & Gaming Magazines

www.cardozabooks.com

3 GREAT REASONS TO VISIT NOW!

1. FREE GAMING MAGAZINES
Go online now and read all about the exciting world of poker, gambling, and online gaming. Our magazines are packed with tips, expert strategies, tournament schedules and results, gossip, news, contests, polls, exclusive discounts on hotels, travel, and more to our readers, prepublication book discounts, free-money bonuses for online sites, and words of wisdom from the world's top experts and authorities. Also, you can sign up for Avery Cardoza's free email newsletters.

2. MORE THAN 200 BOOKS TO MAKE YOU A WINNER
We are the world's largest publisher of gaming and gambling books and represent a who's who of the greatest players and writers on poker, gambling, chess, backgammon, and other games. With more than 10 million books sold, we know what our customers want. Trust us.

3. THIS ONE IS A SURPRISE
Visit us now to get the goods!

So what are you waiting for?
www.cardozabooks.com

GAMBLER'S BOOK CLUB
Shop online at the Gambler's Book Club in Las Vegas. Since 1964, the GBC has been the reigning authority on gambling publications and one of the most famous gaming institutions. We have the world's largest selection of gambling books—thousands in stock. Go online now!

702-382-7555
www.gamblersbookclub.com